*f***P**

THE LADD REPORT

Everett Carll Ladd

THE FREE PRESS

THE FREE PRESS
A Division of Simon & Schuster Inc.
1230 Avenue of the Americas
New York, NY 10020

THE FREE PRESS and colophon are
trademarks of Simon & Schuster Inc.

Designed by MM Design 2000 Inc.

Manufactured in the United States of America

10 9 8 7 6 5 4 3 2

Library of Congress Cataloging-in-Publication Data

Ladd, Everett Carll.
    The Ladd report / Everett Carll Ladd.
        p.   cm.
    Includes bibliographical references and index.
        1. Voluntarism—United States. I. Title.
    HN90.V64L33   1999
    361.3' 7' 0973—dc21
                                                98-31380
                                                      CIP

ISBN 0-684-83735-8

For all the Ladds, with love:

Cynthia
Benjamin and Wendy
Melissa and Paul
Corina and David
Carll and Elizabeth
Ryan
Rachael
Kelley
Michelle
Mary and Stanley

"The root of the state is in the family."

Mencius (372–298 B.C.)

In truth, one of the most remarkable circumstances or features of our age, is the energy with which the principle of combination, or of action by joint forces, by associated numbers, is manifesting itself. It may be said, without much exaggeration, that everything is done now by Societies. Men have learned what wonders can be accomplished in certain cases by union. . . . You can scarcely name an object for which some institution has not been formed. Would men spread one set of opinions, or crush another? They make a Society. Would they improve the penal code, or relieve poor debtors? They make Societies. Would they encourage agriculture, or manufactures, or science? They make Societies. Would one class encourage horse-racing, and another discourage traveling on Sunday? They form Societies. . . . This principle of association is worthy the attention of the philosopher, who simply aims to understand society, and its most powerful springs. . . . That this mode of action has advantages and recommendations, is very obvious. . . . Men, it is justly said, can do jointly what they cannot do singly.

William Ellery Channing,
"Remarks on Associations,"
Christian Examiner, September 1829

If some public pleasure is concerned, an association is formed to give more splendor and regularity to the entertainment. Societies are formed to resist evils that are exclusively of a moral nature, as to diminish the vice of intemperance. In the United States associations are established to promote the public safety, commerce, industry, morality, and religion. . . . The Americans make associations to give entertainments, to found seminaries, to build inns, to construct churches, to diffuse books, to send missionaries to the antipodes; in the manner they found hospitals, prisons, and schools. . . . There is no end which the human will despairs of attaining through the combined power of individuals united into a society. . . .

Alexis de Tocqueville,
Democracy in America, vol. 1, 1835

CONTENTS

ACKNOWLEDGMENTS

Each time I've completed a book I've found myself with a long list of unpaid debts. Authors often get valuable help from many quarters, and I've never been an exception. In this instance—*The Ladd Report*—I owe expressions of deep appreciation to an unusually long cast. The task of assembling the data on which I report was especially demanding, and many people contributed to it.

In May 1996, my colleagues and I at the Roper Center for Public Research began to put together an issue of our magazine, *The Public Perspective*, on what had become a controversial issue, the state of America's civic engagement or "social capital." Contributing editor Karlyn Bowman had first suggested that someone needed to begin a careful compilation and assessment of data bearing on this topic—and why not us? The result was a special issue of the magazine: "A Vast Empirical Record Refutes the Idea of Civic Decline." It prompted a far greater response than any subject we had examined previously in what was then the magazine's seventh year.

One of those responses came from Bruce Nichols, Senior Editor at The Free Press. He urged me to finish what I started—to push the research much farther than was possible in one issue of a magazine and write a book that would deal exhaustively with the argument that America was losing its status as a nation of joiners, the nation that Alexis de Tocqueville had celebrated in *Democracy in America*; and that it was instead retreating into private regardedness. I accepted the invitation.

The necessary exploration could not have been completed were it not for a number of pioneering efforts that brought together survey data on the subject. In particular, I want to acknowledge the importance of the information collected by the National Opinion Research Center of the University of Chicago in its annual study, the General Social Survey. Also of great importance are the extensive surveys done every two years by the Gallup Organization for a leading association that monitors voluntarism and philanthropy, the Independent Sector. A number of other associations had begun to address civic engagement thoughtfully in their surveys, and the work done by ABC News and the *Washington Post* proved especially helpful. Research conducted by the World Values Study Group helped put the U.S. position in comparative perspective. I want to express special appreciation to Juan Diez-Nicolas, President of Analisis Sociologicos Economicos y Politicos, Madrid, Spain, a key member of the World Values Study team. Ongoing research done under the direction of Lester Salamon and Helmut K. Anheier for the Johns Hopkins University comparative nonprofit sector project also helped greatly in locating the U.S. position in civic engagement cross-nationally.

Lots of other data needed to evaluate America's civic health and involvement had never been assembled. Colleagues assisting me in tracking down this information from original sources are Karen Orfitelli, who directed the survey of PTAs and PTOs, Roper Center senior research librarians Rob Persons and Lisa Parmelee, graduate research assistant Regina Dougherty, and my research associate of many years, Marianne Simonoff. Janice Berriault produced many of the book's extensive tables and charts.

I owe an enormous debt of appreciation to five friends and principal collaborators in this project:

- Seymour Martin Lipset, Hazel Professor of Public Policy, George Mason University, for his seminal work on American society in comparative perspective, which did much to frame my approach to the study.

- Bruce Nichols, Senior Editor at The Free Press, who as I've noted first suggested the book, and whose steady hand and insight have guided it from idea to finished manuscript.

- Karlyn Bowman, Resident Fellow of the American Enterprise Institute for Public Policy Research, who first recognized the importance of an inquiry designed to get the facts straight on the condition of civic America; who contributed extensively to Chapter 5, "Social Confidence and Trust"; and who read the entire manuscript in prepublication form and suggested how to make it better.

- Cathy Cuneo, my Administrative Assistant at the Roper Center, who produced the electronic versions of all the prose sections of the book and contributed much to their editing.

- Lynn Zayachkiwsky, Manager of Publications at the Roper Center, who designed all of the tables and charts, and who searched the Web for "fugitive data" needed to secure many of the arguments made in this volume.

- *The Ladd Report* is dedicated to my family—to all the Ladds, who have given me the love and support we all need, and without which any accomplishments we might make would be impossible.

E. C. L.

Mansfield, Connecticut

CHAPTER 1

COUNTING
OUR SOCIAL CAPITAL

THE UNITED STATES is an individualist democracy. "Let government do it" has never been our thing. We've counted on individuals doing it—by accepting responsibility for building and maintaining a good society.

Somewhat paradoxically, an individualist democracy is unusually dependent on harnessing collective or cooperative energies. Individual citizens can't manage a society—can't possibly address its manifold needs in any satisfactory fashion—through solitary labors. We must come together in associations large and small where we learn and practice *citizenship*. Our ideal has been and remains an America of active civic and social organizations, churches, philanthropies, and voluntarism—not just to help concretely with a myriad of social needs and problems but, even more important, to sustain vibrant community life. That the "me" will become too insistent, at the expense of the "we," is a persistent American worry. And engaging citizens in civic affairs is the persistent American answer to how a narrowly self-serving individualism can best be avoided.

No one has ever thought it would be easy, though. A "collectivist" individualism built around community engagement can release enormous civic energy, but it asks a lot of millions of citizens. It's not surprising that many in each succeeding generation of

1

Americans have worried that vigorous community participation through groups and charities and voluntary service is somehow losing ground.

THE TWILIGHT OF CIVIC AMERICA?

These worries are very much evident today. The U.S. economy is hugely successful, but isn't "community" suffering even amidst these burgeoning material resources? Aren't we too transfixed by what *I need*, to make *me* happy, at the expense of what *we need*, as in our family life, for real individual fulfillment? Aren't we losing the level of confidence and trust in one another that's essential to the health of our democracy? Aren't we retreating into private pursuits, or to use a metaphor that has resonated in recent years, aren't we now increasingly "bowling alone"?

Polls pick up the current angst. For example, surveys taken by ABC News and the *Washington Post* regularly ask respondents if they think "things in this country are generally going in the right direction, or . . . have gotten pretty seriously off on the wrong track?" Much of the time large majorities answer that we're heading the wrong way: 57 percent said this in late summer 1997, even though the economy was doing nicely, compared with just 39 percent who thought the country was moving in the right direction. The *Los Angeles Times* had asked this same question in a 1995 survey and got similar results—55 percent said we were off on the wrong track, only 35 percent that things were on the whole moving positively. What's most instructive, when the newspaper's pollsters followed up by asking those who had said the country was somehow going the wrong way rather than progressing why they felt this way, 50 percent talked about crime, family breakdown, and a weakening of religious commitments and standards (while just 19 percent mentioned anything to do with the economy).[1]

Such concerns are often expressed in terms of our "social capital" account. The traditional reference to capital involves economics, of course. My dictionary defines the term as "the wealth, whether in money or property, owned or employed in business . . ."; and as "any form of wealth employed or capable of being employed in the production of more wealth." Drawing on this root, "social capital" encompasses any form of citizens' civic engagement employed or capable of being employed to address community needs and problems and, in general, to enhance community life. The Great Social Capital Debate addresses this question: Are we spending down our supply of social capital? Many think that the balance is now dangerously low and worry about the consequences.

Are we right to so worry? In the pages that follow I will argue that the answer is yes from one important perspective, but an emphatic no from another. Social capital *is* crucial, and it's undergoing some major changes of form. But at the same time, an extensive record shows that we're building up our supply of social capital, not depleting it.

The Ladd Report explores in full detail the web of private sector, voluntary participation in groups or associations, highly organized or informal, to advance common goals and shared interests. The book is about, then, the status of contemporary American citizenship. In examining the level and character of our engagement, I seek to avoid the excesses of both Pollyanna and Cassandra. Are current trends in fact shifting against us, forcing us to, in effect, run uphill in civil life? Or instead, is the ground now sloping, at least a bit, in the direction all friends of civic America would wish? The reader will find here, I hope, guidance on this matter from the head rather than from the heart.

I've assembled and assessed the empirical record on the current state of the country's civic engagement. After examining in Chapter 2 various claims advanced in the debate of recent years, I review in Chapter 3 what we actually know about trends in America's associational life. The Elks and the Boy Scouts are less prominent and active now than they were a half century ago; but the Sierra Club is much more so. Bowling leagues are down, but U.S. Youth Soccer has emerged *de novo* and engages more than two million boys and girls, together with an army of adult volunteers. Individual groups matter to their devotees—but it's the health of the forest that's really important, not that of each tree. What's the health of our forest of civic associations?

Chapter 4 then looks at forms of citizens' involvement that are more demanding than mere group membership—the volunteering of time and labor to work with others for community causes and to meet community needs, and contributing financially to these ends. In Chapter 5, I shift from the contemporary record of civic participation to a key element that underlies it—the degree of citizens' trust in those with whom we must work if we are to enhance the quality of American life, and our confidence in the social and political structure that is the setting for our activities.

Finally, in Chapter 6, I look at how American civic life compares with that of other industrial democracies. A century and a half ago, Alexis de Tocqueville saw America's liberal, individualist democracy as being open to many popular excesses. But he also believed it generated enormous civic energy—by encouraging an unprecedented sense of responsibility among individual citizens for social improvement, and an active, richly pluralistic community life. An exception in the way it had come to experience modernity, America stood out, Tocqueville thought, in the reach of its idea of citizenship. Where do we stand in cross-national comparison now on the eve of a new century?

This book seeks, then, to round up, measure, and analyze our civic health. I hope that, upon reviewing the record, readers will conclude that I've achieved in some substantial measure what I intended to do when this project began: let the data themselves argue the case. If civic America is being eviscerated or at the least weakened appreciably, each of us and those who come after us will inevitably reap the unfortunate consequences. On the other hand, if the country's civic life isn't declining, but rather churning, transforming itself to meet modern conditions without losing positive energy, we should acknowledge it and get on with the task of building upon the new. An insipid nostalgia, which looks to a past that never was and laments the absence of a perfect present which can never be, can only detract from constructive effort.

You will decide for yourself what the record shows. My own conclusion, from two years of rummaging through the assembled findings, is that we have allowed our persistent anxieties about the quality of our citizenship to blind us to the many positive trends that have been occurring. What emerges ringingly from the diagnosis presented here is that civic America is being renewed and extended, not diminished, and that the new era—here in the United States but worldwide as well—will be more participatory, not less so. And this is happening despite such challenges as both Mom and Dad's having to juggle the demands of jobs outside the home with the critical tasks of child-rearing—or as Mom's having to do it all alone. And it's happening in the face of the supposedly narcotizing effects of television.

The engagement of individual citizens in a vast array of groups and voluntary service and charities is generating social capital as never before. This capital is now being spent to meet community needs in every town and city in America. If we better understand what's already being done, we will be energized to do even more. Publics are less likely motivated by alarmist calls that the sky is falling than by the sober assurance that they are doing much that's right. In any case, when it comes to civic engagement it's just not true that the sky is falling. The stars are in their place, and the sky is pretty bright.

CHAPTER 2

NATION OF LONERS?

The Great Social Capital Debate

I WAS WAITING in line for a cup of coffee at a gourmet coffee wagon near my office when a hand patted my back and a voice boomed out: "So what do you think about 'Bowling Alone'?"

It was a distinguished colleague, not in the social sciences, who had just finished reading commentary on Robert Putnam's work, in particular on the argument advanced in his famous article.[1] It wasn't exactly the spot for an extended seminar on America's "social capital." I replied briefly that while I agreed entirely with Putnam (and many others) that the health of the country's associational life and individual participation in civic affairs is of vital importance, I didn't think Putnam was right in claiming that the data show civic decline. "Well, I don't know about the data," my friend replied, "but what he has to say feels right to me, right here." At that he gently patted his abdomen.

The Ladd Report wasn't written primarily as a response to Robert Putnam. Though his essays have received enormous attention, "bowling alone" has seemed to many a powerfully evocative metaphor for a set of worries—diffuse but substantial—about the health of contemporary citizenship. My University of Connecticut colleague is hardly alone in feeling that America's participatory civic life has fallen into sad disrepair. Instead of the nation of joiners so often celebrated in the past, we are, in this view, fast becoming a nation of loners. "Bowling alone" has become the widely accepted shorthand for these concerns. I take issue with Robert Putnam's essay, but only as one among many voices making similar claims.[2]

A huge literature exists on this point. From February 1, 1987, through April 1998, in the Lexis-Nexis compendium of published articles, one finds approximately 1,800 references to social capital (only 130 references in the previous decade); over 950 to civic participation (none in the previous decade); and about 175 to excessive individualism (only 16 in the previous decade).[3] And where these subjects are dealt with substantively, the commentary is heavily negative in its depiction of prevailing conditions. The preponderance of these articles take for granted that civic America is in decline.[4]

To be sure, some work has expressed skepticism about the argument. Neal Peirce, a journalist widely applauded for his reporting on the political cultures of the fifty states, reviewed the outpouring of commentary and asked whether "there [is] danger [that] such analyses tilt toward unreasonable negativity." He decided that they do. "They describe an America different from the country of spirited civic work, proliferating neighborhood development corporations, urban and youth self-efforts, efforts of regional strategic planning, that I encounter in my reporting."[5]

Peirce quotes Brian O'Connell, who was the first president of Independent Sector, an organization that charts and seeks to encourage voluntarism and other civic participation. O'Connell described a citizenry much of which is actively engaged: "We organize to fight zoning changes, approve bond issues, oppose or propose abortion, improve garbage collection, expose overpricing, enforce equal rights, or protest wars. In recent times, we have successfully organized to deal with the rights of women, conservation and preservation, learning disabilities, conflict resolution, Hispanic culture and rights, neighborhood empowerment. . . ."[6] In many respects, we are still much as we were in Tocqueville's day. Why, then, is the "Bowling Alone" thesis so popular?

THE ASTONISHING APPEAL
OF THE IDEA OF CIVIC DECLINE

Nicholas Lemann argues that the "decline" side of the debate over civic America has gained notoriety because it so much accords with the actual experience of many in the social stratum paid to assess these matters. "I have lived," he writes, "in five American cities: New Orleans, Cambridge, Washington, Austin, and Pelham, NY. The two that stand out in my memory as most deficient in the [civic] virtues—the places where people I know tend not to have elaborate hobbies and not to devote their evenings and weekends to neighborhood meetings and activities—are Cambridge and Washington. The reason is that these places are the big time. Work absorbs all the energy. It is what people talk about at social events. Community is defined functionally, not spatially: It's a professional peer group rather than a neighborhood. Hired hands, from nannies to headmasters to therapists, bear more of the civic-virtue load than is typical." Lemann concludes that "to people living this kind of life, many of whom grew up in a bourgeoisie provincial environment and migrated to one of the capitals, the 'bowling alone' theory makes sense, because it seems to describe their own situation as well. It is natural for people to assume that if their own life trajectories have been in the direction of reduced civic virtue, this is the result not of choices they have made, but of a vast national trend."[7]

The idea that Americans are retreating from civic engagement has also gained acceptance because it is serviceable for liberals and conservatives alike. Liberals who think we need more effective government programs to assist and then engage citizens, especially those who have been left behind, and conservatives who believe government has grown too much and now discourages individual initiative, can both accept the thesis.

It's possible, I believe, and in fact essential, to examine trends in civic America without reference to the disagreement about the role of government. Unfortunately, this hasn't happened. Many who have written about the health of contemporary citizenship have insisted on tying their arguments to the liberal-conservative debate. Theda Skocpol writes, for example, that while she accepts "Putnam's broad finding of a generational disjunction in the associational loyalties of many American adults, starting around the mid-1960s," she faults him for giving aid and comfort to right-of-center critics of big government. She insists that "Tocqueville romanticism . . . not only undergirds right-wing versions of the civil society debate, but also influences aspects of Putnam's research. Of course Putnam does not share [Newt] Gingrich's hostility to the welfare state. Yet he often speaks of social capital as something that rises or declines in a realm apart from politics and government."[8]

Skocpol argues that, in fact, the most vigorous and successful of twentieth-century volunteer efforts have stemmed from governmental action or, at the least, encouragement. "Organized civil society in the United States has never flourished apart from active government and inclusive democratic politics."[9] She thinks that the voluntary federations of this century "were often built from the top down," citing as examples the American Farm Bureau Federation (encouraged by the U.S. Department of Agriculture) and the PTA (which grew out of the Congress of Mothers, "knit together from above by elite women" and modeled on the U.S. Congress).

We will continue to differ on how much government the United States should have, and what it should do. But it's silly to describe associational America as a creature of governmental action. Consider, for example, churches. We built into our Bill of Rights prohibition of "established" churches; the government may *not* get involved in founding or institutionalizing a church. Surely the flourishing of all sorts of religious organizations in America is the product not of government action but of *deliberate inaction*.

Many conservatives, too, accept the argument that the United States' social capital is eroding—though they attribute it to government's doing too much. Columnist George Will laments the weakening of a sense of individual responsibility for social conditions. The problem will find remedy, he suggests, only when government backs off and gives the private sector generally, and volunteer associations in particular, more room to operate. Will sees it as axiomatic that "conservatives who worry about the 'sociology of virtue' and the 'ecology of liberty' believe that swollen government, which displaces other institutions, saps democracy's strength. There is, these conservatives believe, a zero-sum transaction in society: As the state waxes, other institutions wane. . . ." He concludes that there's a pressing need to rescue "the little platoons" of voluntary civic engagement from "the federal government's big battalions."[10]

Will echoes an argument that Tocqueville advanced in the second volume of *Democracy in America*. Tocqueville foresaw a time when "man will be less and less able to produce, by himself alone, the common necessities of life." Government's role is likely, then, to expand steadily. "The more it stands in place of associations, the more will individuals, losing the notion of combining together, require its assistance: These are causes and effects that unceasingly create each other."[11] Many have made variants of this argument in our own day, portraying the state as a monolith that eviscerates associational life.[12]

Whether in Hitler's Germany or Stalin's USSR, the totalitarian state was indeed the avowed enemy and exterminator of independent associations of all kinds. These groups had to be crushed because they stood against the mobilization of individuals into the total state by providing independent bases for participation and independent resources for collective action.[13] But Americans have avoided any semblance of totalitarianism. Arguments derived from totalitarian experience are largely irrelevant to our liberal society. Nonetheless, some conservatives concerned by what they see as excessive governmental growth seem at times to have blurred this fundamental distinction, leading them to accept the civic decline thesis uncritically.

If active national government is essential to civic participation, then conservative attacks on government are civically detrimental. If, on the other hand, the country's social capital erodes as government expands, liberals' defense of an expansive state is the culprit. So far as I can tell, the relationship in the United States between levels of governmental activity and the extent and quality of group participation, voluntarism, and philanthropy has in fact never been established. We just don't know what the former's impact on the latter has been. My guess is it's been minimal, because Americans have always retained ample opportunity and incentives for personal participation. Our record with voluntarism and associational activity has probably rested largely on the political freedoms protected by the U.S. constitutional system, and on persisting features of American political culture.

COMMUNITARIANISM

If some in both the liberal and conservative camps have found the civic decline thesis helpful in advancing their broader political agendas, so have others across the political spectrum. Communitarians are a case in point. John Brandl, who teaches at the University of Minnesota's Hubert Humphrey Institute of Public Affairs and espouses a communitarian perspective, describes it as "the conviction that humans are more appropriately understood not as autonomous individuals but as social creatures, whole only in groups and when devoted to others in those groups." He notes that "the critique of liberalism from contemporary communitarian philosophers is that community is necessary for the good life, but liberalism has given us instead loneliness and anomie. . . . Community is necessary for the generation of virtue but, turned loose to follow our base inclinations, we have become dissolute."[14]

Brandl maintains that liberal individualists err in dismissing the problem on the grounds that in a free country people can choose community if they want to. "Communitarians note that Americans are not so choosing. They are divorcing or eschewing the commitment of marriage altogether, leaving the churches, becoming less neighborly, neglecting their children, diverting their eyes from the homeless. . . . Here we see a prefiguring of what could happen to the whole society as communities languish, moral constraints no longer bind, and the whims of the unaffiliated rule."[15]

Individualism, American style, has always been a two-edged sword. It encourages people to make and do and create through their own individual energies, but it runs the risk of becoming narrowly self-serving. However, where is the support for Brandl's assertion that Americans are "leaving the churches"—at a time when religious experience is witnessing enormous vitality in a host of denominations and many newcomers to the religious scene? Are we really becoming "less neighborly," or are we in fact redefining the shape of our "neighborhoods," from clusters of contiguous dwellings to those of shared outlook and interest across religious, political, professional, and social experience? Communitarians have largely ignored such questions, perhaps because acceptance of the idea of civic decline adds urgency to their agenda.

UNDERESTIMATING THE RESOURCES

Robert Woodson, the founder and president of the National Center for Neighborhood Enterprise, has often expressed acute frustration at the failure of the press and other observers to recognize the extent of volunteer activity to meet community needs within the inner city. He has described numerous successful efforts generated within these communities to combat crime, curb the use of drugs, and make neighborhoods more attractive places to live and raise children.[16] Through long engagement on the front lines, Bob Woodson is acutely aware of the ferocious problems many central cities and their residents face, but he is also aware of, and documents, the great resources even these troubled areas derive from the individualist energies of American society. *The Triumphs of Joseph* is a call to recognize these resources better and to take steps to enlarge them.

Political theorist Michael Novak looks at a very different dimension of American society, but makes a similar argument. He discussed how the individualist energies accruing from American ideas and historic experience have fueled extraordinary economic achievements. "For Americans, it is natural to think that the cause of the wealth of nations is inventiveness. American laws, American traditions, American customs, American habits—all are geared toward innovation. The world Americans live in is awash with new products and new services, new machinery, new devices. . . . It is no surprise . . . that the 5 percent of the world's people represented by the population of the United States raises more than half of all the world's venture capital."[17]

Novak argues that American-style individualism is such a major resource for change that benefits the broader community because it is in fact organized around the premise that the individual can't succeed apart from a successful community. "Many analysts go awry," Novak observes, "in arguing that under the capitalism of the Rhine [German or Continental style], the collective is preeminent, whereas under Anglo-American capitalism there prevails the jungle of the anarchic individual. On the contrary, in America the argument nearly always centers on the general welfare, and when a majority can be persuaded that a special interest is hurting too many others, its entitlements are almost certain to be renegotiated."[18] Peter F. Drucker, the distinguished social theorist, makes much the same assessment. There is in the United States, he has written, "a fundamental belief in the individual, his strength, his integrity and self-reliance, his worth in the American tradition. But this 'individualism' is much less peculiar to this country—and much less general—than its (usually overlooked) collectivism. Only it is not the collectivism of organized governmental action from above. It is a collectivism of voluntary group action from below."[19]

Some four decades ago, political scientist Edward Banfield examined the profound difference between an attention to needs that focus narrowly on the immediate interests of the individual and his family, and one that looks further and sees the individual's success inextricably tied to that of the society. Banfield studied civic life—or more precisely, the lack thereof, in a small village in southern Italy. He reported upon an "inability to concert activity beyond the immediate family" as stemming from a social ethos he called "amoral familism."[20] In the type of society he observed in this village south of Naples, Banfield argued, "no one will further the interest of the group or community except as it is to his private advantage to do so. In other words, the hope of material gain in the short run will be the only motive for concern with public affairs. This principle is of course consistent with the entire absence [in this community] of civic improvement associations, organized charities, and leading citizens who take initiative in public service."[21]

The American tradition of "collectivist individualism" that Tocqueville, Drucker, Novak, and many other observers have described stands in sharp contrast to the one Banfield depicted. The American tradition has directed its energy to individual interests narrowly construed, but also to those that can be advanced only in a broader social context. The current debate on the health of civic America has, I believe, suffered from too little recognition of the strength and persistence of our "collective individualism" as a civic resource.

MEASUREMENT PROBLEMS

The difficulty in marshaling systematic data on the vitality of contemporary citizenship has given sensationalizers a huge opening. When it comes to charting U.S. economic performance, we have all sorts of information systematically gathered and carefully maintained. Even so, there have been continuing arguments—both intellectual and partisan—on whether the economy is progressing, regressing, or whatever. It's hardly surprising, then, that so much of the literature on civic performance is riddled with unsubstantiated claims: Apart from all of the other problems standing in the way of balanced assessment, we haven't had anything approaching a comprehensive database on trends in civic life.

If you want to know a major league baseball player's batting average against left-handed pitchers in games completed after

11:00 P.M., you can get it in a flash. But if you want to document what's been happening to associational membership, be prepared to spend a lot of time assembling the material yourself. We know that many Americans give of their time and energy to help others, and that many did the same in 1950, 1900, etc. But is the proportion who volunteer increasing or decreasing? And is the product of our volunteer efforts expanding or contracting?

Levels of philanthropy, something that I and many other observers consider a key indicator of civic engagement, themselves present measurement problems. Americans give to a huge assemblage of groups and causes, operating at all levels of society, whose programs are highly decentralized. Charting philanthropy over time also confronts the difficult task of relating what's given to the financial status of the population—in particular, to what people have left over after their "basic" (itself an evolving idea) needs have been met. Yet, for all these difficulties, data have been gathered more regularly and precisely on charitable giving than on any other areas of civic engagement.

Measurement problems are far thornier when it comes to trends in associational life. Putnam argues that we should be concerned that membership in the Jaycees, Elks, the League of Women Voters, and the PTA has dropped off significantly over the last three decades. It has indeed declined from post–World War II highs in all four of these organizations—as has membership in a host of other groups. But unless one is prepared to argue that a particular organization is uniquely valuable in civic terms, what is one to make of its losing ground? Why should we care that the Benevolent and Protective Order of Elks (BPOE) has fewer members now than in the 1950s? Social and civic groups have come and gone since the beginning of the republic. Putnam offers no evidence—nor do other civic-decline-thesis proponents—that the loss of Elks and Jaycees has not been matched, or even surpassed, by increases in other groups equally attractive in their social/civic reach. Unless one is especially partial to the National Congress of Parents and Teachers, commonly known as the PTA, an organization headquartered in Chicago with state and local affiliates around the country, why should one care that PTA membership today is well off its early 1960s levels? As we will see, a variety of measures show parental involvement in school activities increasing, not decreasing. While PTA membership has declined, that of unaffiliated parent-teacher groups—often called parent-teacher *organizations,* or PTOs—has soared.

The League of Women Voters has seen its membership drop from a high of just over 155,000 to about 82,000. But as these numbers indicate, the League was never a mass-membership organization. Its influence has always derived from sources other than numeric strength—for example, managing events at which candidates present themselves to voters, from local "candidates' nights" to national presidential debates. The League hasn't become less active in these areas. More to the point here, though, is the fact that there has been a proliferation of new women's organizations and growth in many older ones. Some of them are confined largely to the world of Washington-based or state-capital lobbying, but many have active local affiliates. As women have entered the work force in greater numbers, local women's groups with a business/professional focus have grown enormously—and many of them have civic improvement goals that extend far beyond the immediate economic interests that brought the groups into being.

League Membership 1930–1997

1930	79,400
1940	48,300
1950	93,100
1960	127,300
1970	155,600
1980	117,200
1990	97,500
1997	82,500

Soroptimist International is a good example of professional women's heightened civic involvement. Its unusual name is from the Latin, *soror* and *optima,* which mean "women" and "the best." Its current U.S. membership is about twenty-four thousand, organized in nearly eight hundred local clubs. Soroptimists are business and professional women who have come together for such community projects as economic and social development, public health, and environmental improvement. In a similar fashion, the National Federation of Business and Professional Women of the United States encourages public policy education and development. It now has more than eighty thousand members nationally, in twenty-eight hundred local organizations.

In the last two decades, business and professional women have become far more involved in electoral politics. A notable case here is EMILY's List, an organization founded in 1985 by just twenty-five women to raise money for pro-choice women Democratic candidates. EMILY is an acronym for "Early Money Is Like Yeast," and since its founding EMILY's List has become one of the country's biggest contributors to federal candidates. In 1996, it gave $6.7 million to women candidates on the Democratic side.

America's associational life is extensive, diverse, and decentralized—which makes it hard to sort out trends. As I've struggled with the data, I've often felt like I'm drowning in a sea of anecdotes. There are so many different stories—and inevitably they don't all point in the same direction. These difficulties acknowledged, the debate over the health of civic America should be resolved by systematic empirical determination. I believe that readers of this book will find that, taken together, the available data provide a reasonably clear picture of trends in our civic engagement—and that the trends show it extending, not contracting, as it finds new forms and outlets.

WHAT TOCQUEVILLE SAW, AND WHAT WE SEE TODAY

Theda Skocpol thinks that the idea of a vigorous citizenry addressing social needs and problems outside of government is simply "Tocqueville romanticism." It's possible, of course, to present civic engagement in sentimental and unrealistic terms, but Tocqueville didn't romanticize things. He did observe that the United States of his day displayed a level and vigor in associational activity surpassing anything in Europe. "Americans of all ages, all conditions, and all dispositions constantly form associations," he wrote. "They have not only commercial and manufacturing companies, in which all take part, but associations of a thousand other kinds, religious, moral, serious, futile, general or restricted, enormous or diminutive."[22] He thought that one type of American association that he called "intellectual and moral" was especially important. The United States had lots of groups pursuing political and economic interests, but Europe, too, had experience with groups such as these. It was in its churches, of great denominational diversity, and other groups committed to social improvement that America stood out.

Independent of government and for the most part reflecting local energy and commitment, the country's churches were, Tocqueville thought, in a sense its foremost political institution. He remarked that while he had no idea how many Americans had a sincere faith—"for who can search the human heart?"—he felt certain that the vast majority deemed religion and active involvement in religious groups of all kinds essential to maintaining democratic institutions. As ordinary citizens were cut loose from the rigid hierarchy of traditional aristocratic societies and given unprecedented opportunities to participate in decision-making, they had to be prepared to be free. "How is it possible that society should escape destruction if the moral tie is not strengthened in proportion as the political tie [hierarchical authority] is relaxed?"[23] Democracy works only when many individual citizens accept moral responsibility for the state of their society.

Tocqueville saw political democracy growing out of experience acquired in the great variety of civil associations—many entirely nonpolitical. "The greater the multiplicity of small affairs, the more do men, even without knowing it, acquire facility in prosecuting great undertakings in common. Civil associations, therefore, facilitate political associations."[24] An individualist democracy requires that many people be trained to participate and accept responsibility for social outcomes. Even when they entirely lack political objectives, then, small groups are a kind of school of democracy.

National political institutions, notably political parties, in their turn provide essential democratic education for narrowly based community organizations. The latter always run the risk of becoming too assertive of their own immediate objectives, too unwilling to compromise. Broad-based political parties teach people that they must join with many others of diverse views if they are to succeed in advancing general programs. "Thus political life makes the love and practice of association more general; it imparts a desire of union and teaches the means of combination to numbers of men who otherwise would have always lived apart. . . ."[25]

Tocqueville's final major argument about Americans' civic engagement was that, somewhat paradoxically, it was spurred, not diminished, by the strength of their individualism. Unless ordinary citizens have an expansive sense of their rights and responsibilities, and are reasonably confident that their society is organized in a way that lets them really make a difference, they are unlikely to bestir themselves. Tocqueville concluded that individualist Americans believed they were obliged to make personal effort on behalf of social amelioration—and that their society was congenial to such efforts. Individuals *should* participate, and when they do *it works.*

Though individualism may become too narrowly self-serving, without a strong, self-confident individualism an expansive idea of citizenship is impossible. This citizen accepts partial ownership and responsibility for the health of his/her society—which can't be exercised passively. There is no need to introduce "romantic" or utopian standards. Tocqueville's argument is simply that active, voluntary participation by large segments of the populace is needed if individualist democracy is to work.

CIVIC AMERICA
AND THE POSTINDUSTRIAL ERA

As I will argue, civic engagement in America is high and in fact increasing. There is good reason for the trend: It is easier to be an engaged citizen in the Information Economy than in an Industrial Economy. Writing in the early 1970s, Daniel Bell described the emergence of the United States (and other economically advanced countries) into a broad new era. He contrasted this emergent "postindustrial" society with its predecessor, arguing that whereas "industrial society is the coordination of machines and men for the production of goods," postindustrial society is "organized around knowledge." The key developments defining postindustrialism, Bell concluded, are "the exponential growth and branching of science, the rise of a new intellectual technology, the creation of systematic research through R&D budgets, and . . . the codification of theoretical knowledge."[26] The technological revolutions of the postindustrial age have also dramatically expanded wealth. Thus postindustrialism extends the resources for civic participation. It increases dramatically the proportion of the public given advanced educational skills and new communications tools. It frees broad segments of the populace from grinding physical toil. By extending material abundance, it widens the range of individual choice and invites millions to explore civic life in ways previously out of reach for them.

Lester M. Salamon and Helmut K. Anheier have been examining trends in civic participation cross-nationally, as part of the Johns Hopkins Comparative Non-Profit Sector Project. They have found what one would expect from the coming of postindustrial society. They see the planet experiencing a social revolution of enormous importance—albeit one that "is still largely hidden from view, obscured by a set of concepts that cloud its existence and by statistical systems that consequently fail to take it into account."

That innovation is the civil society sector, the plethora of private, non-profit, non-governmental organizations that have emerged in recent decades in virtually every corner of the world to provide vehicles through which citizens can exercise individual initiative in the private pursuit of public purposes. If representative government was the great bureaucratic invention of the eighteenth century, and bureaucracy—both public and private—of the nineteenth, it is organized, private, voluntary activity, the proliferation of civil society organizations, that may turn out, despite earlier origins to represent the greatest social invention of the twentieth century.[27]

That's a large claim. Yet, it would be surprising if the primary precipitating achievements of the late twentieth century—improved material conditions for many, greater educational opportunities, expanded communications resources, and much more political freedom—hadn't extended civic participation in many countries. The U.S. experience, so different in Tocqueville's day from elsewhere, is becoming less dissimilar now. While Tocqueville emphasized the unique way in which America experienced modernity—distinguished by an incredibly rapid extension of individualist norms and institutions—he thought that all nations would eventually encounter it. He wrote that "it seems to me beyond a doubt that sooner or later we, like the Americans, will attain almost complete equality of conditions." Of course, "I certainly do not draw from that the conclusion that we are necessarily destined one day to derive the same political consequences as the Americans from the similar social state." Still, if each nation would move from the old order to the new on its own course, each would in fact experience the new, like it or not. An individualist revolution would sweep the planet, in stages, bringing with it civic involvement by ordinary people far beyond anything open to them historically. The only question—and it was a big one—was how successfully all this would be managed.

As Salamon and Anheier note, in our own day few agencies and research groups have tried to track the extension of individualism systematically. Its cross-national manifestations have been passed over in the face of more dramatic developments, such as the USSR's collapse—even though communism's decline accrued in large part from the spread of individualist norms and aspirations.

A variety of factors have, then, allowed the debate on the health of civic America to amble along inconclusively: "He says, she says, how do you feel about it?" Enough. Interpretations of complex sets of social data are bound to vary some, but the empirical record here is large enough, and strong enough, to effectively take a lot of the issues in the debate off the table. Let's see what we know pretty securely about the present status of our nation of joiners, about the status of our social capital account.

CHAPTER 3

FROM BOWLING LEAGUES TO SOCCER NATION

Churning, Not Decline

ONE REASON THE idea of declining civic engagement has seemed plausible is easy to see: Many older groups have in fact lost ground. Robert Putnam notes that membership or participation is down significantly in Lions Clubs, Shriners, Jaycees, Elks, Masons, the League of Women Voters, the Federation of Women's Clubs, the PTA, labor unions . . . and bowling leagues. Of course, membership is down even more dramatically in the Grand Army of the Republic (GAR), easily the largest social/civic group in post–Civil War America; and in the Anti-Saloon League, an association which energized millions of Protestant Americans in towns across the country in an effort, for a time successful, to make prohibition the law of the land.

Granted, the factors that caused the demise of the GAR and the Anti-Saloon League predated by many decades the drop in Jaycees and Elks. But groups have always come and gone, for many reasons. Membership declines become worrisome only when they're widespread, or if limited, when the groups in retreat are highly important civically and aren't being satisfactorily replaced. If the PTA lost half its members and other parent-teacher associations did not fill the gap, or if the PTA's decline reflected a growing unwillingness of parents to join with others in support of school programs and improvements beyond what's good for Amy and Christopher, that would point to a troubling loss of social capital in at least one key area. But, is that the case?

We will see in this chapter that there has been in fact no loss of parental engagement in school affairs. And this reflects the general pattern. Important changes are occurring in group life—but not decline. Many civic groups in America are further decentralizing. "Devolution" has come to them far more forcefully than to government. In addition, lots of new groups have emerged, crowding out some of the players of earlier eras. Environmental organizations are one example of groups on the rise. Soccer leagues are another. Churches, long a primary part of the country's associational experience, continue to evolve in response to changing styles of religious expression and social needs.

First, though, a word about labor unions. Including them in a list of groups losing members heightens the sense of declining participation. But do organized labor's troubles have anything at all to do with the country's civic health? There's a huge literature on unions' loss of membership since their high point in the 1950s. They boasted 17.7 million members in 1953, 34 percent of nonagricultural employment. In 1995 they had just 16.4 million, 14 percent of workers outside agriculture. Various explanations have been offered for this huge decline— ranging from more sophisticated business resistance to unions, to ineffective labor leadership, to transformations of the contemporary work force, to growing prosperity. But nowhere does one find the argument that workers are now less inclined to join unions because their civic engagement has atrophied.

Most union members really weren't ever engaged in union affairs anyway. Advocates of the civic decline thesis argue that increased membership in organizations such as the American Association of Retired Persons (AARP) shouldn't be taken as an indicator of civic involvement, because most "members" do nothing more than send in modest annual dues and get a slick magazine. Such membership may in fact be nominal, and not to be confused with real civic participation. But if this argument is valid, it must be applied to labor unions. Many unionists come to that status through union shop agreements. I'm currently a member of the labor union that represents University of Connecticut faculty; my membership is obligatory. Even for those who believe they benefit from the representation labor organizations provide them, the idea of a vibrant civic life at the union locals' headquarters is pure fiction. If we are to attend seriously to the question of whether group participation is hurting, we must do more than compile membership lists. The composite story of citizens' engagement is the only point at issue.

CHURNING, NOT DECLINE: THE CASE OF PARTICIPATION IN ENVIRONMENTAL GROUPS

The rise of interest in a cleaner and healthier environment and the spread of commitments to it across large segments of the population are among the most striking political developments in contemporary America. When John Kennedy assumed the presidency in 1961, an environmental movement was nowhere to be seen at the general public level; by the mid-1970s, however, it was full-blown. Reviewing the huge shift in public sentiment on this issue, Karlyn Bowman and I wrote that "on occasion a value that was not politically salient or central comes to be seen as essential. . . . '[T]he environment' made this transition over the 1960s and 1970s. In the postindustrial era large majorities of American citizens across class and other social group lines are deeply committed to a safe, healthful, and attractive environment—and are prepared to support a variety of actions that seem reasonable in promoting those ends."[1]

A survey taken in September 1996 by Roper Starch Worldwide, a prominent survey organization, found 9 percent of respondents describing themselves as active environmentalists and another 62 percent as sympathetic to environmental concerns, compared with 24 percent neutral on these matters and just 4 percent unsympathetic. The National Opinion Research Center's General Social Survey (GSS) in 1994 reported 28 percent of respondents having signed at least one petition on environmental issues in the previous five years. This shift in public opinion on environmental questions is convincingly documented in an abundance of other poll data.

But what about actual involvement by the public in groups dedicated to environmental causes? Is there a shift in participation paralleling the large one in public opinion? It might be that civic involvement in this area has changed little, and that instead energetic issue entrepreneurs in Washington and state capitals have simply taken advantage of shifts in public sentiment to carry the day before legislatures and regulatory bodies.

In fact, the growth of membership in environmental groups and participation in their activities parallels the shift in public opinion. Founded in 1892, the Sierra Club is the oldest of the major environmental organizations. For most of its history it was an "elite" group—with a limited membership of (generally) high socioeconomic status. As late as 1970, the club's membership nationally totaled just under 115,000 (Figure 3.1). Over the next two decades, though, when civic America was supposedly in retreat, Sierra Club membership climbed more than fivefold. Other environmental groups, including the National Audubon Society, the Wilderness Society, the World Wildlife Fund, and the Nature Conservancy, all experienced similar large gains. As Figure 3.1 shows, some of these groups have lost members in the 1990s—perhaps as a result of increased confidence, shown by poll data, that impressive environmental gains have been made and are reasonably secure. Even so, current membership stands at levels far above that of fifteen years ago. A Peter Hart Research survey done in December 1994 found 13 percent of respondents nationally saying they belonged to two or more environmental groups, while another 10 percent belonged to one. Similarly, a 1996 survey taken by the University of Virginia's Center for Survey Research for the American Association of Retired Persons recorded 13 percent of respondents as stating they had been members of environmental groups during the past year.

In "Bowling Alone," Robert Putnam asserts that the growth of environmental organizations doesn't reflect a significant increase

Figure 3.1   Environmental Organizations Have Seen Enormous
Membership Growth

Sierra Club (1892)		National Audubon Society (1905)	
1970	114,336	1970	104,676
1980	181,773	1980	311,269
1990	629,532	1990	548,523
1996	550,000	1996	570,000
Wilderness Society (1935)		World Wildlife Fund (1935)	
1970	N/A	1970	N/A
1980	50,000	1985	172,000
1990	404,000	1991	1,000,000
1996	300,000	1996	1,200,000
Nature Conservancy (1951)		Greenpeace (1971)	
1978	60,000	1971	250
1980	99,000	1980	250,000
1990	578,000	1990	2,500,000
1996	830,000	1996	1,690,500

Source: Membership figures received from organizations' headquarters. Date below name indicates date of founding.

in rank-and-file participation. "For the vast majority of their members, the only act of membership consists in writing checks for dues or perhaps occasionally reading a newsletter. Few ever attend any meetings of such organizations, and most are unlikely ever (knowingly) to encounter any other member. The bond between any two members of the Sierra Club is less like the bond between two members of a gardening club and more like the bond between any two Red Sox fans (or perhaps any two devoted Honda owners)."[2]

Survey analyst George Pettinico explored this question for the Roper Center's bimonthly magazine, *The Public Perspective*. He concluded that "Putnam, and others who hold this view, are mistaken. While certainly not all members of environmental groups are as active as others, far more than a mere 'few' are deeply involved in their organizations. In fact, a closer examination of the green movement in the United States reveals a vibrant, grassroots culture involving countless individuals who are actively engaged in their communities. On almost a daily basis, a plethora of meetings, social gatherings, hikes, bike trips, clean-up projects, rallies, nature workshops and the like are held in communities across the nation by local chapters of national environmental organizations, as well as ad hoc community groups."[3] The Sierra Club is national in scope and does its share of Washington lobbying, but it also has active grassroots organizations. Its Los Angeles chapter, for example, includes sixteen local groups in the Los Angeles area. Pettinico describes the activities of these groups on just one weekend in May 1996: "Twenty-one day hikes (including one for singles only), two evening hikes, three bicycle trips (one for singles only), one bird watching walk, four trail repair outings, a nature camera excursion, a wilderness first aid workshop, a nature knowledge workshop, a backpacking class, a camp fund-raiser, two weekend-long camping trips, and one weekend trip to Catalina Island."[4] "Bowling Alone," indeed!

Pettinico found much the same thing with other environmental organizations. The Audubon Society emphasizes local participation and has over five hundred chapters across the country. Connecticut has 14 chapters with roughly ten thousand members. Pettinico interviewed Patty Pendergast, the Audubon Society's representative for Connecticut, who described the active social life and environmental activities of these local groups. She identified a "core, sociable group" within the local chapters—an experience consistent with that of earlier social and civic associations. Groups have always had different layers of involvement. I found especially interesting Ms. Pendergast's description of the active informal networks that have grown up around shared interests in nature and environmental causes. Speaking, as an example, about those with a special fondness for bird-watching, she observed that "if there is a rare bird sighting, there is a whole core of people who call each other to pass on the information. . . . This is a community of people who know each other, run into each other, rely on each other."[5]

FUNCTIONAL SUBSTITUTION: THE CASE OF PARENTS AND THE SCHOOLS

Of all of the assertions of a decline in civic participation made in recent years, one of the most troubling is that involving the National Congress of Parents and Teachers. Data provided by the organization's national headquarters in Chicago show that the number of parents in local chapters plunged from the early sixties through the early eighties. Membership reached a high of 12.1 million in 1962 and then began falling off, slowly at first but rapidly in the late 1960s and throughout the 1970s. It reached a modern-day low in 1981 of just 5.3 million—a drop in just twenty years of 6.8 million parents (Figure 3.2). Since most of us agree with Robert Putnam that "parental involvement in the educational process represents a particularly productive form of social capital," the PTA's experience deserves examination.

A few factors immediately give pause to the idea that PTA's membership troubles reflect an erosion of social capital. For one thing, note what's happened since the early 1980s. PTA membership nationally has by no means regained anything approaching its high mark, but it has climbed by roughly 1.7 million (1982 to 1996). If the steep decline of the earlier years is a disheartening indicator of eroding social capital, then the substantial gains in recent years should be a heartening sign of recovery. More important, a number of national surveys showed parental involvement in school affairs high and, if anything, increasing over the span when PTAs were declining.

The real reason PTA membership fell off wasn't that parents stopped participating; *rather, they associated increasingly with groups other than the PTA.* That is, they substituted other groups for the same

Figure 3.2   The PTA Story: Membership Down Sharply, 1962–1982; Up, 1982–1996

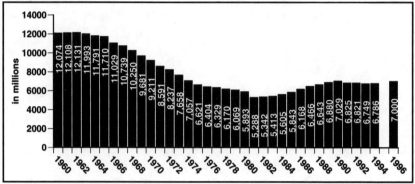

Source: National PTA unpublished data.

basic functions. This was a big deal for the PTA, and for those who believe that its lobbying efforts are important. But it has nothing to do with developments in civic America. Months after I began puzzling over the PTA story, I discussed it with Harry O'Neill of Roper Starch Worldwide. He noted that in the New Jersey community where he lived, the local parent-teacher groups had decided not to disband but to disaffiliate from the national PTA—largely to keep for local use the large portion of dues going to the national and state headquarters. When I related O'Neill's assessment to my wife, she reminded me that when she was an officer of our local Mansfield, Connecticut, PTA in the late sixties, the group voted to become independent—calling itself a parent-teacher organization, or PTO.

The PTA's loss in O'Neill's New Jersey hometown, and in Connecticut, certainly did not represent a lessening of parental involvement. But how typical, in fact, were parents' decisions in these two communities of what was happening across the United States? Highly so, it turns out. In the 1960s and 1970s, huge numbers of local parent-teacher groups disaffiliated from the national PTA. They then took on a great variety of different names, but a large majority became PTOs.

Figure 3.3 shows that by the mid-1990s, less than one-fourth of all public and private K-12 schools had PTA affiliates—ranging from lows of just 4 percent of schools in Massachusetts, 7 percent in Wyoming, 8 percent in Vermont, and 9 percent in Nebraska to highs of 48 percent in Virginia, 51 percent in Maryland, and 72 percent in Utah. On its face it was unlikely that in education-conscious Massachusetts only one school in twenty-five had a parent-teacher group. Something else had to be happening.

There's a political argument over the cause of the PTA's decline. Critics of the organization charge it with becoming a "lapdog of the teachers' unions." According to them, the National Education Association and the American Federation of Teachers have, in effect, taken over the PTA and shaped its political agenda. This has allegedly turned off large numbers of parents.[6] It's clear that many prominent education activists are mad at the PTA for its stands on issues like vouchers and school choice—which the PTA opposes vigorously. But for many parents, "controlling things ourselves right here in town" and keeping all the dues money for local use are probably more important factors leading them to disaffiliate.

How many of the schools without PTAs in fact have no parent-teacher organization at all, or at least none in which parents are much engaged? That was a hard question to answer because no one collects data on PTOs or other unaffiliated parent-teacher groups. We had to conduct our own survey. Covering all fifty states was not possible given our resources, but doing a careful study in a couple of states was. I picked Connecticut—my home state, the country's most affluent, and one with high education levels and a highly urban population. For the other state I picked Kansas, in the agricultural Midwest, which has a demographic profile sharply different from Connecticut's in income, educational background, ethnicity, and occupation. In both these states we drew a random 10 percent sample of all state-accredited private and public schools and contacted their principals' or superintendents' offices. We then conducted telephone interviews to find out what (if any) parent-teacher organizations operated in these schools. We received outstanding cooperation from local officials and

Figure 3.3   The PTA Is Now a Minority Player
(Only One-Fourth of Public and Private Schools Are PTA-Affiliated)

	Number of public schools	Number of private schools	Total number of schools	Number of schools with PTA affiliates	Percent of schools with PTA affiliates
U.S. Totals	86,221	26,093	112,314	26,152	23%
Grades K–12					
Northeast					
Maine	733	140	873	91	10%
New Hampshire	458	130	588	91	15
Vermont	394	85	479	37	8
Massachusetts	1,831	648	2,479	87	4
Rhode Island	308	112	420	52	12
Connecticut	1,045	360	1,405	258	18
New York	4,130	1,985	6,115	1,494	24
Pennsylvania	3,190	1,846	5,036	576	11
New Jersey	2,295	878	3,173	836	26
South					
Delaware	182	90	272	107	39
Maryland	1,263	522	1,785	902	51
West Virginia	883	145	1,028	167	16
Virginia	1,851	515	2,366	1,131	48
Kentucky	1,374	296	1,670	576	34
Tennessee	1,554	496	2,050	344	17
North Carolina	1,968	463	2,431	934	38
South Carolina	1,094	297	1,391	446	32
Georgia	1,767	580	2,347	802	34
Florida	2,733	1,262	3,995	1,295	32
Alabama	1,309	410	1,719	458	27
Mississippi	1,018	221	1,239	296	24
Louisiana	1,459	458	1,917	304	16
Arkansas	1,073	179	1,252	282	23
Oklahoma	1,824	190	2,014	428	21
Texas	6,465	1,353	7,818	2,606	33

Figure 3.3   (continued)

	Number of public schools	Number of private schools	Total number of schools	Number of schools with PTA affiliates	Percent of schools with PTA affiliates
Midwest					
Ohio	3,812	1,016	4,828	907	19%
Michigan	3,432	1,075	4,507	567	13
Indiana	1,912	619	2,531	312	12
Wisconsin	2,030	954	2,984	340	11
Illinois	4,195	1,347	5,542	939	17
Minnesota	2,100	542	2,642	252	10
Iowa	1,554	290	1,844	259	14
Missouri	2,234	719	2,953	446	15
North Dakota	623	59	682	67	10
South Dakota	827	96	923	88	10
Nebraska	1,419	223	1,642	153	9
Kansas	1,491	206	1,697	290	17
West					
Montana	899	82	981	111	11
Idaho	608	78	686	91	13
Wyoming	411	35	446	33	7
Utah	728	66	794	572	72
Colorado	1,460	391	1,851	274	15
Arizona	1,136	263	1,399	259	19
New Mexico	715	166	881	102	12
Washington	2,064	486	2,550	872	34
Oregon	1,213	250	1,463	243	17
Nevada	421	58	479	153	32
California	7,821	3,145	10,966	3,842	35
Alaska	498	66	564	131	23
Hawaii	242	121	363	112	31

Source: Data on the number of public and private K-12 schools are from the U.S. Department of Education, National Center for Education Statistics. The data on the number of local schools affiliated with the PTA are from the National Headquarters of PTA in Chicago. The private school data are for 1993–94, the public school data, for 1994–95—in each case the latest available. The PTA data are for 1995.

completed interviews at more than 90 percent of the schools in our original samples.

We found that virtually all the schools had parent-teacher associations that officials said were active. These officials described concretely the work being done. Their descriptions of the activities belie any claim that we have entered an era of "schooling alone." In both states the preponderance of the parent-teacher groups aren't affiliated with the PTA (or for that matter, with any other body). By far the largest share of unaffiliates call themselves PTOs, but in Connecticut, with numerous Catholic schools, "Home and School Associations" are also common. In Kansas some groups call themselves "Parents in Education" and "Parent-Teacher Groups" (Tables 3.1 and 3.2).

"PTA" is still a shorthand reference for the entire range of parent-teacher organizations. In fact, the PTA isn't the primary association of parents and teachers any longer; it's now a minority player. But because "PTA" is still the widely accepted shorthand, we have had the confusing case of surveys showing enhanced levels of "PTA involvement" in school affairs, even though formal membership in the organization was declining, or holding at levels far below 1960s highs. Surveys taken by the Gallup Organization for Phi Delta Kappa found the proportion of parents of public school children saying they had attended "a PTA meeting" over the past school year up from 36 percent in 1983 to 49 percent in 1994 (Figure 3.4).

This confusion in terminology aside, all the surveys show the proportions of parents saying they have recently attended meetings dealing with local school needs and programs up over the last two to three decades. The Gallup/Phi Delta Kappa surveys report big increases in such parental engagement as meeting with schoolteachers and administrators and attending school plays or concerts. In 1969, just 16 percent of parents told Gallup that they had attended a school board meeting; in 1995, 39 percent said they had (Figure 3.4). Other polls show this same upward progression of involvement from different angles. For example, a June 1978 survey by CBS News found 56 percent of respondents saying their parents never participated in "PTA activities," while only 34 percent said that they themselves never

Table 3.1 But It's Not That Parent-Teacher Groups Are in Decline: In Connecticut, Most Parents' Groups Active in Schools Aren't PTA-Affiliated

AUTHOR'S NOTE: Staff of the Roper Center reached a random sample of 115 K–8, state-accredited schools—public and private—in Connecticut. There are in all 1,066 such schools; we drew a random 10% sample. Principals' and superintendents' offices were then contacted for each selected school and asked what forms of parent-teacher organizations operated in their schools. What follows are the distributions given in these telephone interviews.

	N	%
PTA	26	23
All independent, nonaffiliated groups	87	76
PTO	54	47
Home and School Association*	13	11
PAC (Parents and Children)	2	2
Other	18	16
No formal group	1	1
Refused	1	1
Total *N* = 115		

*"Home and School Association" is the Catholic school equivalent of PTO. "Other" includes 18 organizations each found in only one of 18 schools. Examples—"Parent Activity Club," "Principal's Advisory Committee," "Parents' Association," "Parent Council," etc.

And These Parent-Teacher Groups Are Active: What They Do

	N	%
PTA	26	23
In-School Volunteers		
General classroom and office help	68	59
Library volunteers	36	31
Computer room volunteers	18	16
Reading/literacy volunteers	10	9
Lunch room volunteers	9	8
Fund-raising (book fairs, magazine drives, bake sales, fairs, etc.)	46	40
Field Trips	23	20
Social/Cultural/Charity Events and Activities (plays, dances, arts programs, concerts, environmental programs)	21	18
Senior Citizen Volunteers (senior literacy volunteers, grandparents' programs, retired people as classroom volunteers)	9	8

Note: Adds to more than 100% due to multiple responses.

Table 3.2 In Kansas, the Story Is Much the Same

AUTHOR'S NOTE: Staff of the Roper Center reached a random sample of 81 K–8, state-accredited schools—public and private—in Kansas. There are in all 792 such schools; we drew a random 10% sample. Principals' and superintendents' offices were then contacted for each selected school and asked what forms of parent-teacher organizations operated in their schools. What follows are the distributions given in these telephone interviews.

	N	%
PTA	21	26
All independent, nonaffiliated groups	50	62
PTO	27	33
Home and School Association*	4	5
Site Council	4	5
Booster Club	2	2
Other	13	16
No formal group	8	10
Refused	2	2
Total N = 81		

*"Home and School Association" is the Catholic school equivalent of PTO. "Other" includes 13 organizations each found in only one of 13 schools. Examples—"Parents Always Support Schools," "Parents in Education," "Parent, Student, Teacher Organization," "Parent-Teacher Group," etc.

Table 3.2 The Groups Are Active: What They Do

	N	%
In-School Volunteers		
General classroom and office help	75	93
Library volunteers	13	16
Computer room volunteers	8	10
Reading/literacy volunteers	17	21
Lunch room volunteers	10	12
Fund-raising (book fairs, magazine drives, bake sales, fairs, etc.)	44	54
Field Trips	32	40
Social/Cultural/Charity Events and Activities (plays, dances, arts programs, concerts, environmental programs)	43	53
Senior Citizen Volunteers (senior literacy volunteers, grandparents' programs, retired people as classroom volunteers)	3	4

Note: Adds to more than 100% due to multiple responses.

Figure 3.4   Attendance at School Board Meetings Also Up

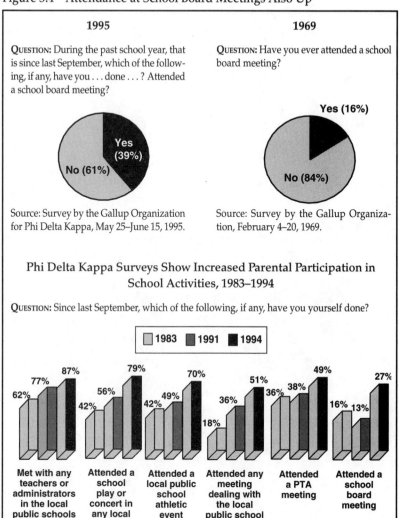

1995

QUESTION: During the past school year, that is since last September, which of the following, if any, have you ... done ... ? Attended a school board meeting?

Yes (39%)
No (61%)

Source: Survey by the Gallup Organization for Phi Delta Kappa, May 25–June 15, 1995.

1969

QUESTION: Have you ever attended a school board meeting?

Yes (16%)
No (84%)

Source: Survey by the Gallup Organization, February 4–20, 1969.

Phi Delta Kappa Surveys Show Increased Parental Participation in School Activities, 1983–1994

QUESTION: Since last September, which of the following, if any, have you yourself done?

☐ 1983   ▨ 1991   ■ 1994

	1983	1991	1994
Met with any teachers or administrators in the local public schools about your own child	62%	77%	87%
Attended a school play or concert in any local public school	42%	56%	79%
Attended a local public school athletic event	42%	49%	70%
Attended any meeting dealing with the local public school situation*	18%	36%	51%
Attended a PTA meeting	36%	38%	49%
Attended a school board meeting	16%	13%	27%

* In 1991, this category was worded: "Attended any meeting dealing with the local public schools."

Source: Survey by the Gallup Organization for Phi Delta Kappa in the years shown. Responses shown for public school parents only.

Figure 3.5   Reported Participation in Parent-Teacher Groups Up Over
Time and Intergenerationally

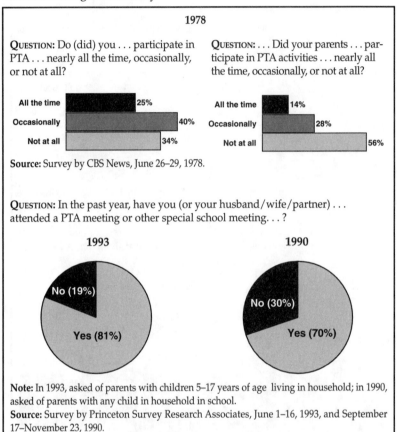

QUESTION: Do (did) you . . . participate in
PTA . . . nearly all the time, occasionally,
or not at all?

QUESTION: . . . Did your parents . . . participate in PTA activities . . . nearly all
the time, occasionally, or not at all?

Source: Survey by CBS News, June 26–29, 1978.

QUESTION: In the past year, have you (or your husband/wife/partner) . . .
attended a PTA meeting or other special school meeting. . . ?

Note: In 1993, asked of parents with children 5–17 years of age living in household; in 1990,
asked of parents with any child in household in school.
Source: Survey by Princeton Survey Research Associates, June 1–16, 1993, and September
17–November 23, 1990.

participated (Figure 3.5). In a 1990 poll, Princeton Survey Research
Associates recorded 30 percent of parents of children aged five
through seventeen as not having attended any PTA or special school
meeting in the past year; three years later, the proportion not attending
was just 19 percent.

Some respondents may, of course, gild their answers to questions like these. The point is that virtually all the studies show higher
proportions indicating that they've participated in school meetings,
organizations, and programs now than in the past. The National
Opinion Research Center's General Social Survey did find a plunge

Figure 3.6   The General Social Surveys Did Find a Decline in Parents' Membership in School Service Groups in the 1970s, but Have Since Shown a Recovery

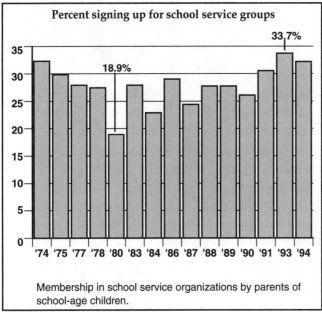

Percent signing up for school service groups

33.7%

18.9%

'74 '75 '77 '78 '80 '83 '84 '86 '87 '88 '89 '90 '91 '93 '94

Membership in school service organizations by parents of school-age children.

Source: National Opinion Research Center, General Social Survey. Surveys conducted in the years indicated.

in 1980 in the percentage of parents of school-age children saying they had joined one or another school service group—but if this drop-off was real it was short-term. NORC surveys in the 1990s have found the proportion of parents belonging to such groups at their highest levels (Figure 3.6).

The organizational side of parental engagement in school affairs may still leave something to be desired, but it shows rising, not declining, levels. Not surprisingly, the preponderance of parents' involvement occurs informally. A survey done by Wirthlin Worldwide in May 1996 found 46 percent of parents of school-age children saying that helping with homework was key to effective parental involvement, compared with just 11 percent attaching that importance to belonging to the PTA (Figure 3.7). Similarly, a study by ABT Associates in 1992 reported 90 percent of parents of children in

Figure 3.7   Parents' Involvement in the Schools Takes Many Forms

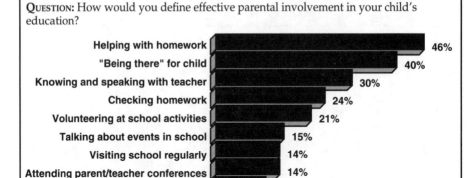

QUESTION: How would you define effective parental involvement in your child's education?

Activity	Percentage
Helping with homework	46%
"Being there" for child	40%
Knowing and speaking with teacher	30%
Checking homework	24%
Volunteering at school activities	21%
Talking about events in school	15%
Visiting school regularly	14%
Attending parent/teacher conferences	14%
Belonging to the PTA	11%
Reading with child at home	10%
Other	9%

Note: Survey is of parents of school-age children only.
Source: Survey by Wirthlin Worldwide for the Education Policy Institute, May 14–17, 1996.

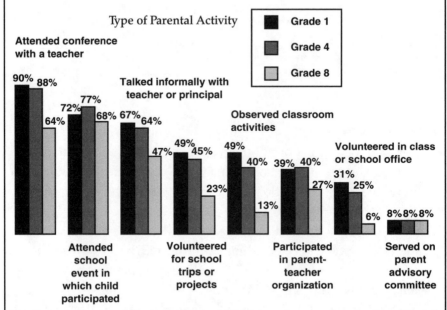

Type of Parental Activity

Grade 1
Grade 4
Grade 8

Attended conference with a teacher
90% 88% 64%

Talked informally with teacher or principal
72% 77% 68%

Observed classroom activities
67% 64% 47%

Volunteered in class or school office
49% 45% 23%

Attended school event in which child participated

Volunteered for school trips or projects
49% 40% 13%

Participated in parent-teacher organization
39% 40% 27%

Served on parent advisory committee
31% 25% 6%

8% 8% 8%

Note: Survey is of parents of school-age children only. Percentages shown are of parents who participated in activities at their children's school at least once in 1992.
Source: Survey by ABT Associates for the U.S. Department of Education, Planning and Evaluation Service, 1992.

grade 1 having attended a conference with their child's teacher and 49 percent having volunteered for a school trip or project; these responses contrast sharply with the 8 percent having served on a parent advisory committee.

It's impossible to measure precisely the extent and variety of parents' engagement in school affairs—whether working with their own children individually or coming together with others in organized activity—to examine curriculum issues, complain about educational programs, or enhance the schools' social and recreational life. Still, it's striking that not one set of systematic data shows a decline in parental involvement, while many show increases. If there's an empirical case for the argument that America's social capital is eroding, the experience of parents and schools doesn't provide it. Instead, the PTO story makes the case for the existence of expansive, energetic local engagement.

BLIND SPOTS: OVERLOOKING THE RELIGIOUS SIDE OF CIVIC AMERICA

The experience of America's churches is an even more impressive example. Churches and other religious bodies seek to guide their members in the worshiping of God, of course, and in living lives that accord with religious precepts. But churches are also civic associations, far and away the largest and most active. Through them tens of millions of Americans meet regularly to participate in an array of social activities that dwarfs those of all other groups. Churches are primary community meeting places. They engage their parishioners in activities to help those who are hurting and to strengthen the larger community. They are, as we will see in the next chapter, easily the major recipients of individual philanthropy. Formal church membership in the United States surpasses that of any other industrial democracy—and it shows no sign of declining, though its denominational makeup is changing radically.

Many Americans tell pollsters that they believe religion is losing

Figure 3.8   Contrary to Some Common Assumptions, the Proportion of Americans Belonging to a Religious Organization Has Increased Sharply Over Time

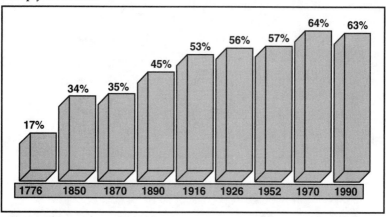

Source: Data based on calculations by Roger Finke and Rodney Stark, *The Churching of America, 1776–1990* (New Brunswick, NJ: Rutgers University Press, 1994), p. 16.

influence in the life of the nation. It's hard to know how to evaluate such oft-stated sentiments. Are respondents mostly just expressing worry about a primary set of values—anxiety being natural with things that really matter? Or do they actually see religious influences in retreat? We do know that the proportion of Americans belonging to a church or other religious organizations has been trending upward over much of U.S. history (Figure 3.8). Roger Finke and Rodney Stark have observed that "this pattern can truly be called the churching of America. On the eve of the Revolution only about 17 percent of Americans were churched. . . . [B]y 1906 slightly more than half of the US population was churched. Adherence rates reached 56 percent by 1926. Since then the rate has been rather stable although inching upwards. . . ."[7]

In the 1990s, between four and five out of ten adult Americans say that they attend church "regularly," meaning almost every week or more often. About two-thirds are members of a church or synagogue. More than a quarter call themselves "very active" participants in their religious bodies, while more than another 40 percent are moderately active. No other organization records anything approaching so high a participation level (Figure 3.9). Even teenagers, who for as long

Figure 3.9   Two-Thirds Say They Are Church Members, and 3 in 10 That They Attend Services at Least Once a Week

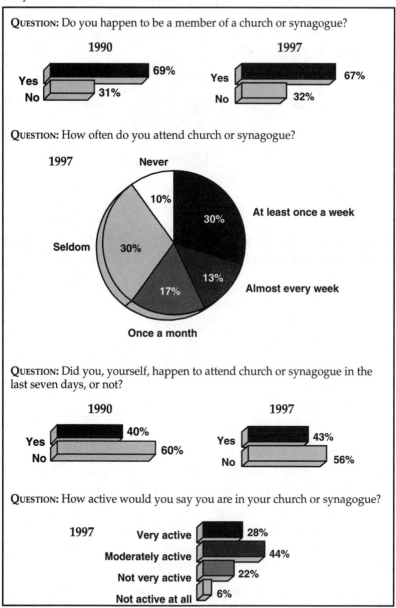

QUESTION: Do you happen to be a member of a church or synagogue?

1990

Yes   69%
No   31%

1997

Yes   67%
No   32%

QUESTION: How often do you attend church or synagogue?

1997   Never

10%

30%   At least once a week

Seldom   30%

13%
17%   Almost every week

Once a month

QUESTION: Did you, yourself, happen to attend church or synagogue in the last seven days, or not?

1990

Yes   40%
No   60%

1997

Yes   43%
No   56%

QUESTION: How active would you say you are in your church or synagogue?

1997   Very active   28%
Moderately active   44%
Not very active   22%
Not active at all   6%

Source: Surveys by the Gallup Organization, June 15–17, 1990, and March 24–26, 1997.

Figure 3.10   Teenagers Now Show High Church Participation

QUESTION: How often do you go to a house of worship? . . .

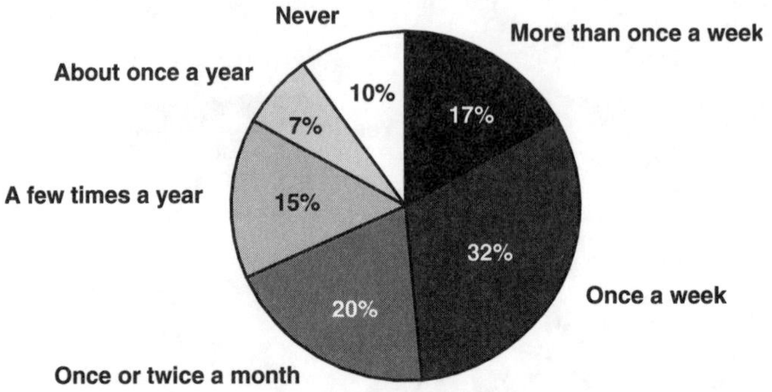

Frequency of Teens' Attendance by Social Background

	Male	Female	Parents Married	Parents Divorced	Protestant	Catholic	White	Non-White
Regularly	46%	50%	51%	35%	58%	54%	48%	54%
Occasionally	22%	18%	20%	22%	21%	24%	21%	12%
Rarely/Never	32%	32%	29%	43%	21%	22%	32%	34%

Note: More than once a week/once a week = "Regularly"; once or twice a month = "Occasionally"; a few times a year/about once a year/never = "Rarely/Never."
Source: Survey of 16–18-year-olds by the Roper Center for Public Opinion Research, University of Connecticut, for the *Reader's Digest*, January 28–February 6, 1997.

as data have been collected have had the lowest church-participation rate of any age group, are significantly involved (Figure 3.10).

While membership and participation in religious groups remain high, and if anything have climbed in recent years, individual denominations are going in opposite directions. Some are growing rapidly, others losing ground. Americans are continuing to "vote with their feet"—moving from one denomination to another to better meet their spiritual and social needs. In the last quarter-century, the old mainline Protestant churches have lost members, while a host of pietist and evangelical denominations have expanded strikingly (Figure 3.11). "Megachurches" have been appearing around

Figure 3.11 As With Group Participation of All Kinds, Some
Religious Bodies Show Striking Gains, Others Big Declines

Winners and Losers in American Church Membership, 1960 to 1995	Membership (in millions)		% Change
	1960	1995	
Total membership	115	159	38
Total resident pop.	180	263	46
Pentecostals	1.9	10.8	469
Jehovah's Witnesses	0.3	1.0	286
Latter-Day Saints	1.6	4.9	197
Adventists	0.4	0.8	132
Mennonites	0.2	0.3	85
Baptists	21.1	36.7	73
Roman Catholics	42.1	60.3	43
Methodists	12.4	14.6	17
Jews*	5.4	6.0	11
Lutherans	8.1	8.3	3
Presbyterians	4.3	4.2	−4
Churches of Christ	4.0	3.7	−8
Episcopalian	3.4	2.5	−26
Reformed/UCC	2.7	2.0	−26
Friends	0.1	0.09	−32
Other	6.4	2.7	

*Data are for 1960 and 1990. Figures represent estimates of membership in an ethnic and social as well as religious community.

Note: The data above do not represent a complete census of U.S. denominations. They derive from membership reports sent in to the yearbooks by the denominations themselves, but as such, represent a summary of membership just about as complete as can be obtained anywhere.

Source: 1962 and 1997 *Yearbook of American and Canadian Churches.*

the country, offering their parishioners social services—such as well-equipped gymnasiums—never before part of the church scene. "Para-religious" bodies like Promise Keepers are engaging millions entirely outside any denominational structure. The widespread contemporary search for new religious forms is also seen in the huge growth of "community churches," which are often intensely participatory but eschew historic denominational associations.[8]

Again, it's important to keep in mind that churches have never been purely religious bodies; they have been centers of social and civic life—and prime centers of volunteering. They are now showing enormous energy in transforming themselves to meet contemporary needs and tastes. Charles Trueheart writes that the Next Church movement is consciously asking "Who is our customer?" and answering that it's people who have been irreligious or unchurched and not responsive to the old-style religion. He describes one Next Church prototype, the Mariners in Newport Beach, California, as "relentlessly creative about developing forms of worship—most symbolically and definingly music—that are contemporary, accessible, 'authentic.'"[9]

> Next Church services are multimedia affairs. Overhead projectors allow the preacher to sketch his point the way a teacher would on a chalkboard, or to illustrate his message with a cartoon, an apt quotation, or a video clip. Lyle E. Schaller, an independent scholar and the author of dozens of books on the large-church movement, suggests that these are the descendants of the stained-glass window, another nonverbal storytelling device. (Overhead projectors are also used instead of hymnals and prayer books, and to project the Scriptures of the day.) A personal testimonial, or a two- or three-person dramatic sketch, illustrates with true-life vignettes the point the pastor is making in his message (it's almost never called a sermon). . . . [10]
>
> No spires. No crosses. No robes. No clerical collars. No hard pews. No kneelers. No biblical gobbledygook. No prayerly rote. No fire, no brimstone. No pipe organs.

No dreary eighteenth-century hymns. No forced solemnity. No Sunday finery. No collection plates.[11]

All this can be jarring for the more tradition-minded; and some of it is undoubtedly both crass and superficial. But little of it fits a picture of Americans retreating into more solitary pursuits, finding their cultural substance primarily through the tube.

A VAST PROLIFERATION OF SMALL GROUPS

The experience with community churches—growing rapidly, entirely decentralized—follows a pattern now evident in many civic groups. The *Dallas Morning News* made a major commitment to explore for its readers civic participation around the country. Its extended series reported on "a dizzying array of community revitalization groups and initiatives."[12] Examples of what was variously described as the "civic revival movement," the "new citizenship," "civic democracy," and "community building" were tracked in roughly fifty metropolitan areas. The work of over eighty nonprofit organizations, foundations, and other community groups was discussed. And all this represented only a drop in an ocean of activity. Many of the organizations cited are themselves "roof organizations" for numerous other bodies (e.g., Alliance for National Renewal—an umbrella for more than a hundred organizations involved in the civic renewal process; Family Support Centers—twenty-two organizations across Maryland). Community development corporations numbered only three hundred in 1980, but today stand at three thousand. The impossibility of measuring at all precisely the growth of local initiatives was exemplified in the failed attempt by a Washington research firm to compile—as part of a study commissioned by the Rockefeller Foundation—"a comprehensive list of local, state and national actors" in the civic revival movement. The task was called "too daunting" by one of the directors.

More than a decade and a half ago, sociologist J. Miller McPherson described the exceptional proliferation of small groups in modern-day America. He found group engagement at such a level that, typically, something on the order of a hundred thousand groups or more operate in a U.S. city of a million people.[13]

In many sectors of national life, the trend is away from centralized, national organizations to those that are decentralized and local.[14] Voluntarism and civic participation evince a degree of devolution that may surpass what's occurring in the governmental sphere. Many civic leaders believe that this expansion of grassroots engagement enhances the efficacy of work being done. Again, though, it's much harder to measure participation that's highly decentralized and local than that which is centralized and national.

Only on occasion is a systematic effort made in a community to describe the extent of civic activity. One such effort is ongoing in West Philadelphia, encouraged by the University of Pennsylvania. It focuses on only the part of the city where the University is located, and hence doesn't chronicle even the entire Philadelphia story. Nonetheless, the range of groups and activity described for West Philadelphia—only a

**Table 3.3 A Vast Proliferation of Community Service Groups:
One Chapter in the (West) Philadelphia Story**

AUTHOR'S NOTE: The listing that follows is only a sample of West Philadelphia civic groups compiled by the Office of Community Relations of the University of Pennsylvania's Center for Community Partnerships, which serves as a liaison between Penn and neighborhood organizations and business and community leaders. Religious organizations are among the hundreds of neighborhood institutions not listed here.

Duplications that appear in these lists reflect the functions that each organization performs in the various community service organizations.

Civic—Center for Literacy; Citizens for Progress; The Declaration of Independence Cosigners Convention; Haddington Leadership Organization; Mantua Against Drugs; Parents Against Drugs; V.O.T.E. (Voice of The Electorate); Walking Against Drugs.

Community Service—ACCESS West Philly; House of Umoja; Independent Community Assistance Network; Intercultural Family Services; Mayor's Office of Community Services; People's Emergency Center; West Philadelphia YMCA.

Immigrant and Refugee Mutual Aid—Cambodian Association of Greater Philadelphia; Ethiopian Community Association of Greater Philadelphia; Greater Philadelphia Overseas Chinese Association; Hmong United Association of Greater Philadelphia; Korean Community Development Services Center; Lao Family Community Organization; Liberian Redevelopment Association; New World Association of Immigrants from Russia in Pennsylvania; Southeast Asian Mutual Assistance Association Coalition (SEAMAAC); Vietnamese United National Association of Greater Philadelphia.

Safety—Landsdown Town Watch of Philadelphia; Squirrel Hill Substation; West Philadel-

Table 3.3 The (West) Philadelphia Story (continued)

phia Partnership Task Force on Safety and Security.

Youth and the Elderly—Belmont Youth Leader; CB's Role Models; Children's Advocacy Center; Haddington Multi-Services for Older Adults, Inc.

West Philadelphia Neighborhood—Belmont Village Civic Association; Cedar Park Neighbors; Cobbs Creek Neighborhood Advisory Committee; Dunlap Community Citizens Concerned; East Mill Creek Community; Garden Court Community Association; Haddington/Cobbs Creek CDC; Haddington Leadership Organization; Lar-Sage Neighbors; Mantua Community Developers; Mantua Community Planners; Mill Creek Council, Inc.; Mill Creek Townhouse Association; New Breed Community Council; Overbrook Civic Association; Overbrook Farms Club; Overbrook Neighborhood Improvement Council; Overbrook Park Civic Association; PFSNI (Penn Faculty and Staff for Neighborhood Issues); Powelton Village Civic Association; Regent Square Civic Association; Spruce Hill Community Association; Squirrel Hill Community Association; Walnut Hill Civic Association; West Philadelphia Partnership; West Powelton Concerned Community Council; Woodside Park Civic Association; Wynnefield Heights Civic Association; Wynnefield Residents Association.

West Philadelphia Community Development Corporations—Fresh Start Community Development Corporation; Habitat for Humanity, West Philadelphia; Independent Community Assistance Network; Peoples Emergency Center; Philadelphians Concerned About Housing; West Philadelphia Partnership Community Development Corporation.

Neighborhood Improvement Organizations—Belmont Improvement Association of West Philadelphia; Belmont United Neighbors; Block Captains Association; Carroll Park Community Council; Cathedral Park Association; Cedar Park Neighbors; Cobbs Creek Neighborhood Advisory Committee; Cobbs Creek Recreation Advisory Council; Dunlap Concerned Citizens; East Mill Creek Community; East Powelton Concerned Citizens; Fresh Start Community Development Corporation (CDC); Fusion Community Development Corporation; Garden Court Community Association; GRASP; Haddington/Cobbs Creek Community Development Corporation; Haverford Norris Civic Association; Housing Consortium for Disabled Individuals; Lar-Sage Neighbors; Mantua Community Developers; Mantua Community Planners, Inc.; Mantua Scattered Sites Tenant Council; Mantua Recreation Center; Mill Creek Council; Mill Creek Townhouse Association; Mount Olive Youth Association; Neighborhood Development Project; New Breed Community Council; Overbrook Civic Association; Overbrook Community Council; Overbrook Farm Club; Overbrook Farms EAST Residence Association; Overbrook Neighborhood Improvement Council; Overbrook Park Civic Association; Parkside Association of Philadelphia; Parkside Historic Preservation Corporation; People's Emergency Center Community Development Corporation; Philadelphians Concerned About Housing; Powelton Village Civic Association; Regent Square Civic Association; Regional Council of Neighborhood Organizations; Saunders Park Neighbors; Sherwood Park Civic Association; Southwest Branch Christian Street YMCA; Southwest Community Enrichment Center; Southwest Community Services; Spruce Hill Community Association; Spruce Hill Garden Club; Squirrel Hill Community Association; United Emergency Service; University City Historical Society; Upper South West United Civic Association; Walnut Hill Community Association, Inc.; West Park Respect Yourself; West Park Tenants; West Philadelphia Coalition of Neighborhoods and Businesses; West Philadelphia Community Center; West Philadelphia Cultural Alliance; West Philadelphia Economic Development Corporation; West Philadelphia Empowerment Zone; West Philadelphia Enterprise Center; West Philadelphia Fund for Human Development; West Philadelphia Partnership; West Philadelphia Partnership Community Development Corporation; West Powelton Concerned Community Council; West Shore Civic Association; Woodland Terrace Home Owner's Association; Woodside Park Civic Association; Wynnefield Heights Civic Association; Wynnefield Residents Association.

small portion of which is summarized in Table 3.3—gives further challenge to the idea that Americans are retreating from civic engagement.

COMPETITION IS A MAJOR FORCE IN THE "GROUP MARKETPLACE," AS IN THE ECONOMY

In case after case where a group that's been important in the past now finds itself losing ground, or at least struggling to maintain its place, investigation shows that the main cause is simply strong competition. The PTA has been getting beat by local entrepreneurs who are more concerned with "hometown" than with Chicago headquarters. The old mainline churches are getting beat by all sorts of religious newcomers. And the Elks and Masons are losing out to the Sierra Club.

Often competition doesn't destroy the old front-runner—it just erodes its old ascendancy. The experience of the Boy Scouts is a case in point. Figure 3.12 follows Boy Scout membership from the early years of this century through 1996. Total membership—the boys themselves as well as adults who participate as volunteers—reached its high in 1970; it has since then declined by roughly 10 percent. To be sure, 1996 membership surpasses that of 1960. And the organization's whopping 1.2 million adult volunteers is by any standard impressive. Similarly, the Girl Scouts report more than 780,000 adult members or volunteers for 1995, down slightly from the nearly 790,000 high achieved in 1992, but far above the last four decades' low point of 1980, when adults volunteering in Girl Scout activities totaled just under 535,000. These data don't indicate that participation in scouting is withering, but they do show that the growth of times past is no longer being obtained.

The reason scouting is struggling to maintain its position is the exponential growth of other youth organizations. Both the Boy and Girl Scouts have encountered in recent years much more competition from other youth groups, which are typically more decentral-

Figure 3.12   Membership in Boy Scouts, 1911 to 1996
(in thousands)

1911	1920	1930	1940	1950
61.5	478.5	847.1	1,449.4	2,795.2
1960	**1970**	**1980**	**1990**	**1996**
5,161.0	6,287.3	4,326.1	5,445.9	5,628.8

Note: Membership figures include scouts as well as leaders who are adult volunteers. In 1996, of the roughly 5.6 million members, about 4.4 million were scouts and 1.2 million were adult volunteers.
Source: Boy Scouts of America, unpublished data.

ized than the scouts. The proliferation of leagues offering organized instruction, parental involvement, and active youth participation in baseball, softball, and soccer illustrates this development. The Little League was established in 1939 by Carl Stolz to keep older kids from beating up on younger ones in his hometown of Williamsport, Pennsylvania. Today, Little Leagues field about three million boys and girls in eighty-eight countries. And it's but one part of a vast effort at youth participation designed to teach athletic skills, encourage discipline and teamwork, and provide fun and social interaction. First and second graders begin with "Tee-Ball," proceed in third and fourth grades through "CAPS," enter Little League formally in grades five and six, and then go on to Pony League. Little League is run on the local level by adult volunteers; the organization has only a hundred full-time paid employees.[15] Little League softball was started in 1974, as was Senior League softball (for girls thirteen to fifteen). Big League softball (for girls sixteen to eighteen) was introduced in 1980.

The progress is much the same in youth soccer. U.S. Youth Soccer now has over a half-million adult volunteers and two and a half million youth players. In just one smallish city, Oswego, New York, the Youth Soccer Association enrolls about five hundred players in both its fall and spring programs. The activity didn't exist at all until 1977.[16] Young Americans are certainly not playing alone. What's more, all this youth activity doesn't occur without serious adult engagement. Writing in the *Atlantic Monthly* about the growth of U.S. Youth Soccer, Nicholas Lemann observes that "as a long-standing coach in this organization, I can attest that it involves incessant meetings, phone calls, and activities of a kind that create links between people which ramify, in the manner described by [Robert] Putnam, into other areas."[17]

SURVEYS OF GROUP MEMBERSHIP AND PARTICIPATION

Research by Sidney Verba, Kay Schlozman, and Henry Brady has found high levels of group membership and participation by adult Americans—entirely consistent with the scenario we have developed from other kinds of data. Nearly 80 percent of adults surveyed by Verba and his colleagues reported that they belonged to at least one association, with religious groups not included; the highest proportion was affiliated with a social service group (Figure 3.13).[18] More people give money to groups like the American Heart Association and the United Way than attend meetings of these organizations or give time to their programs. But in the case of educational, business, professional, sports, leisure, and fraternal organizations, the ranks of those attending meetings surpass those making financial contributions but not otherwise participating.

Another survey, done nationally by the University of Connecticut's Institute for Social Inquiry for the National Commission on Philanthropy and Civic Renewal in 1997, reported much the same high engagement. It found 45 percent of adult respondents saying that they had attended a public meeting on town or school affairs at least once in the past year, 41 percent that they had attended one or more meetings of clubs or civic organizations, and

Figure 3.13   The Survey Story: High Levels of Group Membership and Participation

	All Respondents
Percentage affiliated with at least one association	79%
Percentage affiliated with . . .	
. . . a charitable, social service assoc.	44%
. . . an educational assoc.	25%
. . . a business, professional assoc.	23%
. . . a hobby, sports, leisure assoc.	21%
. . . a service, fraternal assoc.	18%

Type of group	Those who attend meetings	Those who give money, but don't attend meetings
Charitable, social service	14%	79%
Educational	50%	34%
Business, professional	66%	13%
Hobby, sports, leisure	52%	17%
Service, fraternal	50%	35%

Note: The five sectors of organizational activity shown above are those that have the highest levels of participation.
Source: The work is reported on by Sidney Verba, Kay Lehman Schlozman, and Henry Brady in *Voice and Equality: Civic Volunteerism in American Politics* (Cambridge, MA: Harvard University Press, 1995), pp. 58–65.

Figure 3.14   High Group Participation Is the Norm

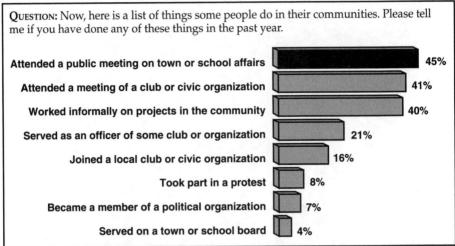

QUESTION: Now, here is a list of things some people do in their communities. Please tell me if you have done any of these things in the past year.

Attended a public meeting on town or school affairs — 45%
Attended a meeting of a club or civic organization — 41%
Worked informally on projects in the community — 40%
Served as an officer of some club or organization — 21%
Joined a local club or civic organization — 16%
Took part in a protest — 8%
Became a member of a political organization — 7%
Served on a town or school board — 4%

Source: Survey by the Institute for Social Inquiry, University of Connecticut, for the National Commisson on Philanthropy and Civic Renewal, March 14–31, 1997.

40 percent that they had participated informally in community projects (Figure 3.14).

A major study of civic engagement conducted in late 1996 by the Center for Survey Research at the University of Virginia for AARP (the American Association of Retired Persons) found the same high level of group membership. Especially interesting are the data on group participation by age. Young adults are much more inclined to join organizations like health and sports clubs and parent-teacher associations than are the elderly, of course, while the latter participate more in church groups, neighborhood associations, and fraternal organizations like the Elks and the Knights of Columbus. But overall, group participation is remarkably even across age lines (Table 3.4). On the other hand, levels of group membership correlate strongly with education. People with graduate degrees report an average of more than ten such associations, compared with an average of just one for those with elementary school training only (Figure 3.15).

Table 3.4 The Survey Story: Group Membership High Among All Age Groups

QUESTION: I am going to read a list of types of organizations, and for each one I would like to know if you have been a member of any such group during the past twelve months.

Percent saying they had been a member in the last year:

	All Respondents	Respondents by Age			
		18–30	31–49	50–70	70+
Religious	61%	48%	61%	69%	74%
Health/Sport/Country Clubs	30	43	32	21	10
Professional or Trade	27	25	34	26	7
PTA, PTO, School Groups	21	15	35	8	2
Hobby/Garden/Computer	19	22	18	17	16
Neighborhood Groups	18	7	21	22	16
Social Clubs	17	21	16	17	16
Health Issue or Disease	16	18	14	18	11
None	14	17	13	11	13
Environmental	13	14	14	10	12
Scouts/Youth	11	11	18	4	4
Literary/Art/Study	11	13	11	10	9
Fraternal Groups (e.g., Elks)	10	6	8	12	20
Labor Unions	10	7	12	11	4
Organizations for Older People	10	2	3	21	26
Other Public Interest	9	9	10	7	7
Political Clubs	9	9	8	9	8
Social Service	8	8	9	9	6
Veterans' Groups	7	3	5	10	16
Support, 12-Step Groups	7	3	5	10	16
Other Civic, Community	5	5	6	5	4
Ethnic/Cultural	5	7	5	5	1
Farm	5	3	4	6	7

Source: Survey by the Center for Survey Research, University of Virginia, for the American Association of Retired Persons (AARP), October 23–December 16, 1996.

Figure 3.15   The Survey Story: Big Differences in Group
Membership by Educational Background

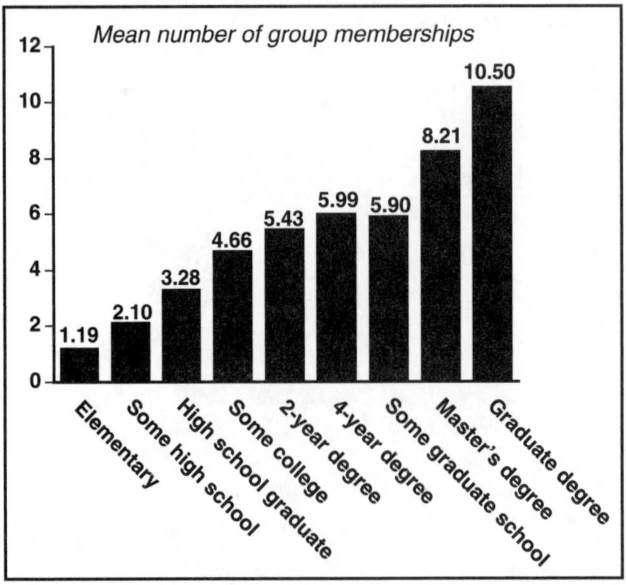

Source: Survey by the Center for Survey Research, University of Virginia, for
the American Association of Retired Persons (AARP), October 23–December 16, 1996.

THE SURVEY STORY: ARE THE NORC FINDINGS AN EXCEPTION?

Robert Putnam cites findings of the National Opinion Research Center's General Social Surveys, which he concludes provide evidence that "at all levels of education and among both men and women, [there has been] a drop of roughly one-quarter in group memberships since 1974."[19] In fact, from the mid-1970s through 1994 (the last year data on this topic were collected), the surveys show the average number of group memberships fluctuating up and down, with no apparent pattern, within a narrow range. The mean number of memberships reported by adult Americans ranged from a high of 1.87 in 1986 to a low of 1.45 in 1991; the 1994 figure stood at 1.61—about the middle of the pack for the span covered by these surveys

Figure 3.16   The General Social Survey Data Show No Consistent Trend in Group Membership Rates Since the Mid-1970s

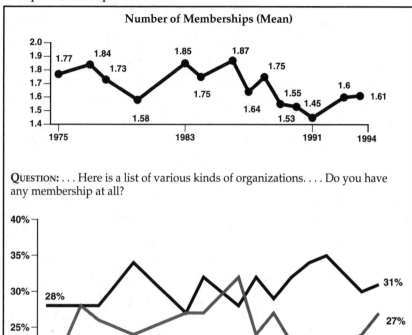

Number of Memberships (Mean)

QUESTION: . . . Here is a list of various kinds of organizations. . . . Do you have any membership at all?

Source: Surveys by the National Opinion Research Center, General Social Survey.

(Figure 3.16). Looking at the data from another angle, the proportion reporting no memberships, or three or more, has also fluctuated with no evident trend over the last twenty-plus years. The percentages reporting no memberships and three or more memberships in 1994 were in the middle range for the span.

Even were the GSS findings a representative study of Americans' group participation, they could not be taken as evidence of decline—they show little change occurring. But the GSS findings are in fact out of step with the preponderance of measures that put associational participation on the rise. In 1988, well before the controversy over civic decline emerged in its present form, two leading social scientists, Frank R. Baumgartner and Jack L. Walker, published a comprehensive account of why, in their view, GSS findings varied from other studies. They cited a number of monographic accounts that point to increased group participation since World War II.[20] Their explanation for the discrepancy between the GSS and other studies was that the GSS's otherwise sensible pursuit of time-series data had put unfortunate limits on the type of information being collected. NORC maintained the trendable categories on its standard question, Baumgartner and Walker concluded, at the cost of missing changes stemming from the appearance of new groups, increases in multiple group memberships, and related developments. They presented their own survey findings, from a revised question on group affiliations, that show much larger proportions joining voluntary associations than NORC surveys found.[21] NORC's Tom Smith, a thoughtful methodologist, defends the NORC standard question, challenging the Baumgartner and Walker account on several methodological grounds.[22] An assessment of these contending interpretations lies beyond my purpose here. I note only that the NORC data for the last two decades show generally stable group membership levels, not declining membership; and that some evidence suggests that the NORC surveys have missed actual increases in group participation because their standard question misses some new groups appearing on the scene.

The key features of postindustrial society—major increases in education and in access to information, freedom from backbreaking physical labor and from subsistence concerns for much of the population, etc.—should be producing a more participatory society. So far our review finds the data supporting the theory. Joining has in fact become more widespread, not less so.

CHAPTER 4

VOLUNTEERING AND GIVING

The Cast Has Changed, but Levels Are Up

JOINING FACE-TO-FACE groups to express shared interests is a key element of civic life. Such groups help resist pressures toward "mass
society" that may inhere in an impersonal, national electronic communications system. They teach citizenship skills and extend social
life beyond the family. They address common problems. Anyone
who has participated much in community associations knows they
can be petty and peevish—but they're essential to a healthy civic
America. As we have seen and will continue to see, group life shows
no signs of withering.

But joining a group isn't the only way to partake of a healthy
civic life. Volunteering is another key aspect of citizen engagement.
And happily, the news on volunteering in America is very good—
contrary to some critics' lament that these days "everything has a
price." Volunteering is up significantly, even among young people. Furthermore, charitable giving—which may not bring the
giver into contact with others, but which is certainly a prime measure of civic commitment—is increasing even among the young.

A huge number of Americans do volunteer work—for all the
demands on two-wage-earner families and the allure of television sit-
coms. ABC News and the *Washington Post* found, in a 1997 survey,

58 percent reporting that in the past year they had volunteered for a church, charity, or other community group—up from 44 percent in 1984, when the same question was asked. Roughly half who claimed they had volunteered said that they do it regularly. That's about a quarter of the entire adult population (Figure 4.1). About four in ten who volunteer got started by a personal invitation to do so. One of the best ways to get more people involved is to ask them.

Other studies show a similar upward progression in voluntarism during the contemporary postindustrial era. Polls done by Gallup and Princeton Survey Research Associates (PSRA) have asked the same question on personal involvement in social service work since 1977, and these data show the percentage of the public thus engaged having roughly doubled over the span (Figure 4.2). Surveys taken by the Roper Center for *Reader's Digest* found 53 percent saying in 1994 they had volunteered at least once over the past year; in 1997 the proportion was 59 percent (Figure 4.3). Changes of this magnitude shouldn't be taken seriously when they occur only in single instances. But when study after study shows the same pattern, and trend lines are clearly etched, we should sit up and take notice. The levels of volunteer service that Americans are now reporting are substantially higher than those reported a decade or two ago.

When CBS News and the *New York Times* asked their respondents whether they had "personally gotten involved in giving your time and energy to a volunteer or community service activity" in the past year or two, 59 percent said yes (poll of January 1997). This survey then sought to "fine-tune" the response by pushing harder: "I mean not just belonging to a group, but actually working in some way to help others for no pay." The proportion now saying they had volunteered dropped—but only modestly, to 49 percent of respondents.

The proportion of the population that volunteers dwarfs that which participates regularly in established civic organizations. The same CBS News/*New York Times* poll of January 1997 that found 49 percent having worked to help others for no pay over the past year reported just 20 percent saying they "regularly attend or participate

Figure 4.1   Surveys Found the Percentage Doing Volunteer Work 14 Points
Higher in 1997 Than in 1984

QUESTION: In the last year or so, have you done any volunteer work for any
church, charity, or community group?

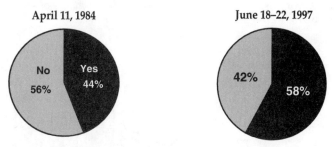

April 11, 1984

No 56%   Yes 44%

June 18–22, 1997

42%   58%

Source: 1997 survey by Princeton Survey Research Associates for the Pew Research Center; 1984
survey by CBS News/*New York Times*.

Asked of those who have ever volunteered

QUESTION: Was that . . . a one-time thing,
or do you do volunteer work on an
occasional basis, or on a regular basis?

QUESTION: . . . Was that volunteer work
for an organized group, or was it something you did on your own?

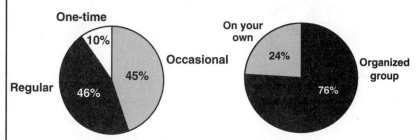

One-time 10%
Occasional 45%
Regular 46%

On your own 24%
Organized group 76%

Source: Survey by Princeton Survey Research
Associates for the Pew Research Center, June
18–22, 1997.

Source: Survey by ABC News/*Washington Post*,
April 21–24, 1997.

QUESTION: Did someone personally invite you to do volunteer work, or did you
read or hear about a need for volunteers, or did you get the idea on your own?

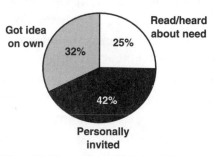

Got idea on own 32%
Read/heard about need 25%
Personally invited 42%

Source: Survey by ABC News/*Washington Post*, April 21–24, 1997.

Figure 4.2   Surveys Show a Large Increase in Social Service Activities Over the Past Two Decades

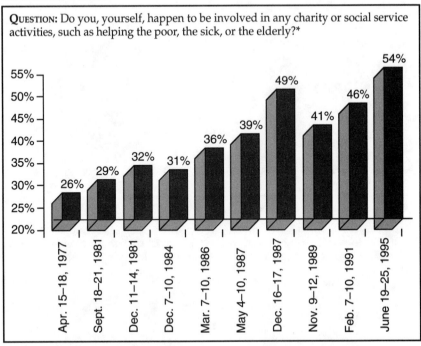

QUESTION: Do you, yourself, happen to be involved in any charity or social service activities, such as helping the poor, the sick, or the elderly?*

*Question wording varies slightly in each asking.
Source: Surveys in 1977–1989, by the Gallup Organization; surveys in 1991 and 1995, by Princeton Survey Research Associates.

in a civic organization or service club, like the Chamber of Commerce, the Kiwanis Club, or the PTA. . . ."

Independent Sector is an organization that monitors voluntarism and charitable giving and promotes these activities. Surveys it has sponsored since 1987 (with the fieldwork done by Gallup) classified 80 million adult Americans as volunteers (45 percent of the population) in 1987 and 93 million as volunteers in 1995 (49 percent of adults). The 1995 study estimated that the average volunteer gave about four hours of his/her time a week, or more than two hundred hours over a year. All of these estimates are, of course, rough approximations. The key finding is that most research shows the proportions of Americans doing volunteer service both high and rising.

Figure 4.3   Recent University of Connecticut Surveys
(Done Nationally) Found Nearly Half Saying They Had Done
Volunteer Work in the Past Year

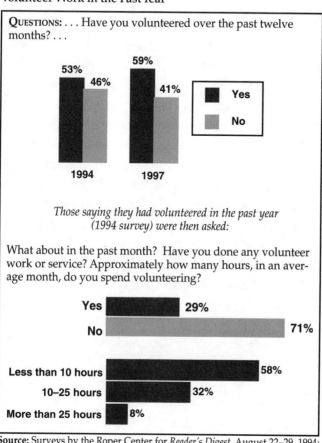

QUESTIONS: . . . Have you volunteered over the past twelve
months? . . .

*Those saying they had volunteered in the past year
(1994 survey) were then asked:*

What about in the past month? Have you done any volunteer
work or service? Approximately how many hours, in an average month, do you spend volunteering?

Source: Surveys by the Roper Center for *Reader's Digest*, August 22–29, 1994;
and by the Institute for Social Inquiry, University of Connecticut, for the
National Commission on Philanthropy and Civic Renewal, March 14–31, 1997.

By any measure the reported rates of voluntarism in the United States are extraordinary. In a study done by Princeton Survey Research Associates in April 1997, 83 percent of all respondents said they had volunteered at least once a month for at least one of a series of civic activities. Presented with a list of nine avenues for voluntarism, just 17 percent said they did not participate regularly in any of them, and just 12 percent volunteered in only one. An extraordinary 29 percent of all respondents said they volunteered regularly in four to six of the nine, and 10 percent in seven or more of these areas (Figure 4.4). The same PSRA survey asked respondents whether they volunteered through (a) a religious organization, (b) a school in the community, (c) some neighborhood organization, (d) groups based in their place of work, or (e) some national organization. Seventy-five percent reported having volunteered through at least one of these facilities—and 20 percent through three of them, and 10 percent through four or five (Figure 4.5).

Alexis de Tocqueville argued in *Democracy in America* that religion had served in this country as a principal ally of political democracy and civic engagement. He noted, for example, how the first public school systems emerged in Connecticut and Massachusetts out of religious commitments. The Puritans insisted that each person needed to be able to read God's word directly through the Bible; and pursuing this they established school systems to achieve universal literacy. "The reader will undoubtedly have remarked the preamble of these enactments: in America religion is the road to knowledge, and the observance of the divine laws leads man to civil freedom."[1] Tocqueville went on to argue that, in sharp contrast to the European experience of the eighteenth and nineteenth centuries, in the United States "liberty regards religion as its companion in all its battles and its triumphs, as the cradle of its infancy and the divine source of its claims."[2]

Modern-day surveys support and amplify Tocqueville's observations. Without exception, to my knowledge, they have found a strong correlation between levels of civic engagement and church attendance. For example, one survey taken by the Center for Survey Research at the University of Virginia in late 1996 found just 29 per-

Figure 4.4 More Than Eight in Every Ten Americans Say They Do Volunteer Work Monthly for at Least One Community Organization

QUESTION: How often, if at all, do you participate in the following volunteer activities . . . ? Do you do this once a week or more, several times a month, about once a month, a few times a year, less often than that, or never?

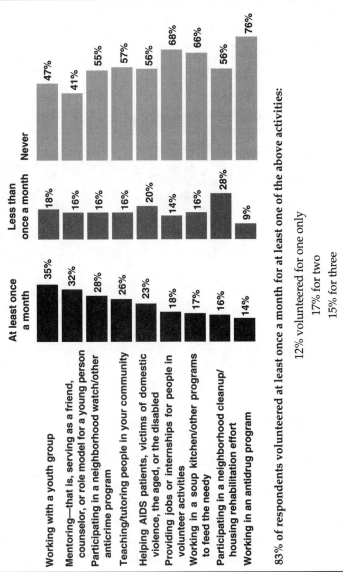

83% of respondents volunteered at least once a month for at least one of the above activities:

12% volunteered for one only
17% for two
15% for three
29% for four to six
10% for seven to nine

Source: Survey by Princeton Survey Research Associates for *Newsweek*/NBC News, April 14–15, 1997.

Figure 4.5   Three-Quarters of Americans Say They Do Volunteer Work Through One or More Principal Groups or Organizations

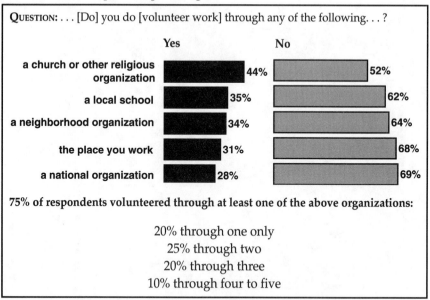

QUESTION: . . . [Do] you do [volunteer work] through any of the following. . . ?

	Yes	No
a church or other religious organization	44%	52%
a local school	35%	62%
a neighborhood organization	34%	64%
the place you work	31%	68%
a national organization	28%	69%

75% of respondents volunteered through at least one of the above organizations:

20% through one only
25% through two
20% through three
10% through four to five

Source: Survey by Princeton Survey Research Associates for *Newsweek*/NBC News, April 14–15, 1997.

cent of those who reported never attending religious services saying they had done volunteer work over the past year, compared with 49 percent of those who attended church weekly and 61 percent who said their church attendance was even more frequent (Figure 4.6).

The wording of questions and other aspects of survey methodology do have some impact, of course, on what levels of volunteering are reported. As Figure 4.7 shows, the less demanding question put by ABC News and the *Washington Post* in their April 1997 survey recorded larger proportions saying they had volunteered (for church groups, schools, environmental cleanup programs, and the like) than did the 1996 National Opinion Research Center's General Social Survey (for similar volunteer activity). The NORC question tries to shake respondents from a casual "Yes, I volunteer" for activities which, in this society, are widely deemed virtuous. (An April 1997 poll done by NBC News and *Newsweek* found 59 percent of its adult

Figure 4.6 Those Attending Church Regularly Are Far More
Likely to Perform Volunteer Service Than Nonattendees

[Respondents were classified as having volunteered on the basis
of their answer to this question.]

QUESTION: Please think of volunteering as help you provide for
free to organizations such as charities, schools, hospitals, religious organizations, neighborhood associations, and civic or
other groups. Have you voluteered any of your time to these
types of organizations in the past 12 months?

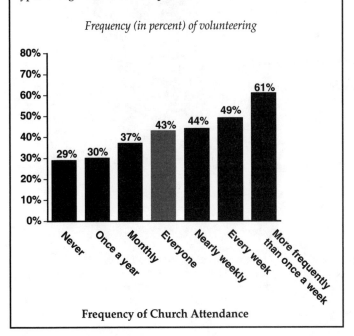

Frequency (in percent) of volunteering

Frequency of Church Attendance

Source: Survey by the Center for Survey Research, University of Virginia for the
American Association of Retired Persons, October 23–December 16, 1996.

Figure 4.7   How You Ask the Question Does Matter: An ABC News/*Washington Post* Survey Found Higher Levels of Volunteer Work Than Did the General Social Survey

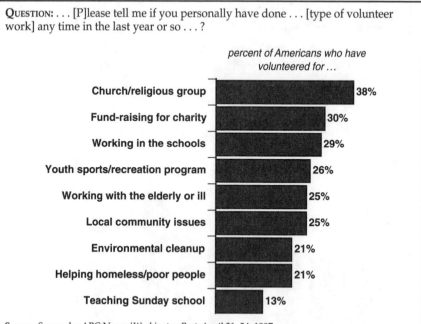

QUESTION: . . . [P]lease tell me if you personally have done . . . [type of volunteer work] any time in the last year or so . . . ?

percent of Americans who have volunteered for . . .

Church/religious group	38%
Fund-raising for charity	30%
Working in the schools	29%
Youth sports/recreation program	26%
Working with the elderly or ill	25%
Local community issues	25%
Environmental cleanup	21%
Helping homeless/poor people	21%
Teaching Sunday school	13%

Source: Survey by ABC News/*Washington Post*, April 21–24, 1997.

QUESTION: Listed on this card are examples of the many different areas in which people do volunteer activity. By volunteer activity I mean not just belonging to a service organization, but actually working in some way to help others for no monetary pay. In which, if any, of the areas listed on this card have you done some volunteer work in the past twelve months?

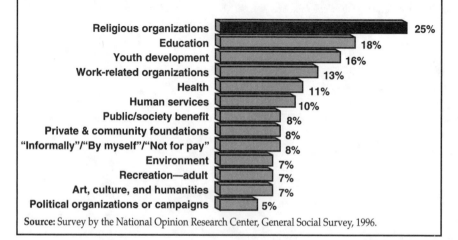

Religious organizations	25%
Education	18%
Youth development	16%
Work-related organizations	13%
Health	11%
Human services	10%
Public/society benefit	8%
Private & community foundations	8%
"Informally"/"By myself"/"Not for pay"	8%
Environment	7%
Recreation—adult	7%
Art, culture, and humanities	7%
Political organizations or campaigns	5%

Source: Survey by the National Opinion Research Center, General Social Survey, 1996.

respondents saying they believe people "have a moral obligation to volunteer for charitable or community service activities.") Yet even with its more demanding question, the 1996 GSS shows roughly six respondents in ten volunteering in at least one area and a third doing so in two or more areas (Table 4.1).

Early in 1997, prior to the convening of the President's "Summit for America's Future" in Philadelphia, the Pew Research Center commissioned Princeton Survey Research Associates to conduct major surveys of volunteer activity nationally and in Philadelphia itself. The Pew research reported levels of activity nationally comparable to what other recent studies have found. As in most central cities, a relatively high proportion of Philadelphia's population needs economic assistance and lives in single-parent households; so it isn't surprising that its rates of volunteering fell below the national average. But participation in Philadelphia was still substantial—22 percent said they had volunteered for one or more organizations to help the poor, elderly, or homeless (compared with 34 percent nationally); 16 percent had volunteered in a school tutoring program (22 percent nationally); and 27 percent had worked without pay for a church or religious group (39 percent nationally).[3]

One of the most interesting findings of the Pew surveys comes from comparison of levels of volunteering for religious and other nonpolitical civic organizations on the one hand and for political activity on the other. The latter lags far behind the former. Church is up; state is down. But this is hardly cause for concern, despite the hand-wringing of some who see government as the center of public life. Politics just isn't as important for most of us as other facets of civic engagement. We settled fundamental issues of how government should be organized a long time ago, and we opted decisively for limited government. With political conflict relatively muted, we feel able to pay little attention to the game of politics much of the time and to instead focus on civic activities that really interest us.

Table 4.1 The GSS Found the Proportion of the Public Who Volunteer Highest Among Those in Their Middle Years, Who Have College Degrees and Above-Average Income, and Who Regularly Attend Church

	Percentage Volunteering for:		
	None	One	Two or More
Everyone	42%	24%	34%
By Gender			
Male	42	27	31
Female	43	22	36
By Age			
18–29 years	44	29	27
30–44 years	35	24	41
45–59 years	38	23	39
60+ years	58	20	22
By Region			
East	53	23	24
Midwest	35	24	41
South	45	25	30
West	35	23	41
By Education			
Less than H.S.	62	24	15
H.S. grad	49	26	25
Some college	38	26	36
College grad	27	16	57
Postgrad	24	25	52
By Income			
Less than $15,000	55	23	22
$15,000–$19,999	51	23	27
$20,000–$29,999	40	28	32
$30,000–$49,999	37	27	36
$50,000–$74,000	31	20	49
$75,000+	31	20	49
By Church Attendance			
Once a week or more	26	25	50
Once a month or more	38	23	39
Several times a year	42	23	35
Once a year or less	50	26	25
Never	63	22	15
By Denomination			
Protestant	40	23	36
Catholic	47	24	29
Jewish	35	21	44
None/other	49	24	˙27

Source: National Opinion Research Center, University of Chicago, General Social Survey, 1996.

THE NEXT GENERATION

Perhaps older folks always worry about the next generation, fearing that it just may not "be up to it"—may not be willing to work hard enough, for example, or may expect too much to come too easily, or may adopt less demanding standards. Yet, the record seems clear that in American experience young people have typically resembled their elders in core values. My earlier research showed that claims of generational distinctiveness—whether for the "twentysomethings," the "boomers," or the "Depression generation"—have often been wildly overstated.[4] As people grow older, they assume new social roles and responsibilities, acquire different interests, experience changing needs. But young Americans differ from their elders in essentially the same way now as in the past. They're just younger.

True generational effects, as opposed to recurring age differences, are weak in most areas of our social and political life. When Gallup asked its respondents in a 1994 survey which they enjoyed more, "the hours when you are on your job, or the hours when you are not on your job?" it found lots fewer eighteen- and nineteen-year-olds than those forty to fifty-nine saying "on the job." But Gallup had asked this same question in 1955 and got the same response pattern. Then, only 30 percent of respondents aged twenty-one to twenty-nine said they enjoyed their on-the-job hours more, compared with 47 percent of those aged forty to fifty-nine and 61 percent aged 60 and older. These age differences don't point to a generational shift in attitudes toward work. Young people simply tend to have less interesting jobs; they've just begun to work their way through their careers. And they have more things they want to do off the job.

It's the same thing with many other social values. The country's religious life is sometimes thought to be caught up in generational shifts. The sixties generation was supposed to be much less religious than its predecessors. But when we have asked people about their religious *beliefs*—for example, whether they believe in God, or the idea of Heaven—we haven't found any significant differences separating the young, the middle-aged, and the old. When we turn to current religion-related *behavior,* such as rates of church attendance, we do find large age differences. Today's youth are less inclined than their elders to describe religion as immediately important to them. But surveys in earlier periods found the same thing. People in their late teens and their twenties typically have been less regular church-goers than those with growing families or than those whose age gives them a more vivid sense of their mortality. We are now seeing a slew of "gee whiz" stories about boomers "returning to church," but the development is in fact just another case of the normal age progression. Boomers are getting older.

In volunteering and other forms of helping others, teens and young adults look much like older Americans, though they get involved in different ways (Figure 4.8). A survey of teenagers done by CBS News and the *New York Times* in April 1998 found 58 percent of them reporting that they had done volunteer work in the past year—"actually working in some way to help others for no pay." They are comparably ready to take individual responsibility through direct engagement. At the same time, as data presented in Table 4.2 (page 76) indicate, young people are less likely to contribute to charities; most of them, of course, haven't yet acquired independent financial means. That young people are less inclined to volunteer their services through community groups (Table 4.1) is also primarily a product of routine age-cycle experience: This activity generally comes later as they settle into their own jobs and family life, independent of their parents. Overall, there's no indication that the "next generation" of Americans is less civic-minded than its predecessors.

Experience with volunteering and other community service reflects a pattern that sociologist Seymour Martin Lipset has described in terms of "the more, the more." He means that the more likely people are to participate in one form of civic activity or another and the busier they are professionally, the more likely they are—despite being busy—to do still more. Along these lines, a 1992 Gallup survey for Independent Sector found that a significantly higher proportion of teenagers holding part-time jobs (65 percent) did volunteer work than teens who had no paid employment (55 percent of whom said they had recently volunteered).

Figure 4.8   Like Older Groups, Young People Get Involved in Many Ways

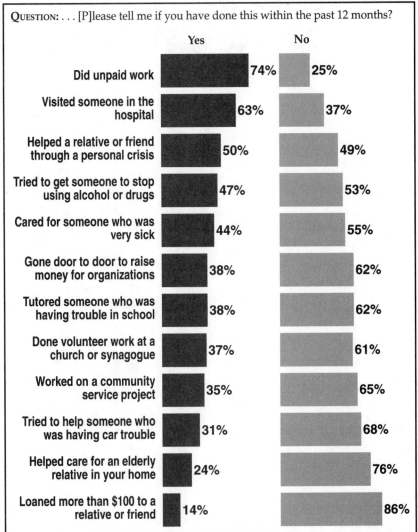

QUESTION: . . . [P]lease tell me if you have done this within the past 12 months?

Yes — No

	Yes	No
Did unpaid work	74%	25%
Visited someone in the hospital	63%	37%
Helped a relative or friend through a personal crisis	50%	49%
Tried to get someone to stop using alcohol or drugs	47%	53%
Cared for someone who was very sick	44%	55%
Gone door to door to raise money for organizations	38%	62%
Tutored someone who was having trouble in school	38%	62%
Done volunteer work at a church or synagogue	37%	61%
Worked on a community service project	35%	65%
Tried to help someone who was having car trouble	31%	68%
Helped care for an elderly relative in your home	24%	76%
Loaned more than $100 to a relative or friend	14%	86%

Source: Survey of young people ages 12–17 by the Gallup Organization for the Independent Sector, 1996.

Table 4.2 Rates of Charitable Giving Also Vary Greatly by Respondents' Economic Status and by Religious Participation

| | *Percentage Giving to:* | | | |
	None	One Group	Two	Three or More
Everyone	28%	28%	18%	26%
By Gender				
Male	29	28	17	27
Female	28	28	19	26
By Age				
18–29 years	45	29	12	14
30–44 years	24	30	18	29
45–59 years	23	23	23	32
60+ years	26	28	19	27
By Region				
East	30	22	19	29
Midwest	29	23	17	31
South	30	30	16	23
West	24	33	20	23
By Education				
Less than H.S.	46	31	12	12
H.S. grad	31	31	19	20
Some college	26	29	21	24
College grad	17	18	18	47
Postgrad	17	25	18	41
By Income				
Less than $15,000	50	31	13	6
$15,000–$19,999	37	29	17	17
$20,000–$29,999	30	32	21	18
$30,000–$49,999	19	29	22	30
$50,000–$74,000	15	24	20	41
$75,000+	10	19	19	53
By Church Attendance				
Once a week or more	13	29	24	33
Once a month or more	23	30	18	29
Several times a year	29	24	16	32
Once a year or less	37	27	13	23
Never	44	27	15	13
By Denomination				
Protestant	26	30	18	26
Catholic	28	24	18	30
Jewish	21	9	18	53
None/other	40	26	19	15

Source: National Opinion Research Center, University of Chicago, General Social Survey, 1996.

DID VOLUNTEERING FALL IN THE LATE SIXTIES AND THE SEVENTIES?

Some organizations like the American Red Cross have found it harder in recent years to recruit volunteer help than they did in, say, the 1950s. But a host of other groups have seen their volunteer ranks increase dramatically. The volunteer program of the Prison Fellowship Ministries has, for example, almost doubled in the past decade. Some older groups thought to have been especially hard hit by the big increase in the proportion of women in the paid labor force have in fact seen volunteering hold its own or even increase. The Girl Scouts are a case in point. They have more volunteers or "adult members" now in the 1990s than in any preceding period. The national office of Girl Scouts of the USA reported roughly 380,000 adult members in 1950, 535,000 in 1980, and 805,000 in 1996.[5] Volunteering in support of Girl Scout activities is higher now than a half century ago, even when population increases are taken into account.

This said, scouting's volunteer ranks were reduced sharply between 1960 and 1980, dropping by roughly 240,000 over the span. Since 1980, the Girl Scouts have rebounded strongly. By itself this might not mean much: Civic organizations are always confronting developments quite special and specific that impact on their membership and participation rates. But the Girl Scout experience seems to be fairly common. Other organizations saw their participation levels drop in the late 1960s and 1970s, only to recover and move ahead again during the past fifteen years or so. Boy Scout membership fell by nearly 2 million in the 1970s; it has since climbed by about 1.3 million. As noted in Chapter 3 (Figure 3.2), PTA membership plunged from the late 1960s through the early 1980s but has since come back significantly—despite the fact that the decision of many local parent-teacher groups to operate independently apparently isn't being reversed. Relatedly, NORC's General Social Surveys reported a decline over the 1970s in the percentage of parents saying they participated in school service groups; again, the low point was reached in 1980 (Figure 3.6). Since then, the percentage of parents participating in school service groups has climbed and was about 13 points higher in 1994 than it had been fourteen years earlier. By a host of different measures, the late 1960s on the one side and the late 1970s or early 1980s on the other seem important boundaries in civic participation.

We lack evidence that firmly establishes this apparent pattern of short-term decline followed by recovery. Much of the systematic collection of relevant data didn't commence until sometime in the 1970s. These data clearly show large gains in participation since the 1970s, but leave us uncertain about what went on before. Still, findings such as those in Figure 4.2 suggest that the 1970s may have been an aberrational decade in which there was a short-term fall in many forms of civic engagement. It's striking that only 26 percent of adult Americans interviewed by Gallup in 1977 said they were involved in any charity or social service activity, whereas the proportion was twice as great (54 percent) when the same question was posed by Princeton Survey Research Associates in 1995.

That these fragmentary findings may point to a real pattern gains credence against the backdrop of the socioeconomic and political experience of the late 1960s and the 1970s. This was a time of growing opposition to the war effort in Vietnam, especially on college campuses across the country. A president was forced to resign amidst the Watergate scandals. The 1970s saw what was for the United States unprecedentedly high inflation, spurred in part by "oil shocks." Motorists found themselves waiting in line for hours to buy gasoline—a commodity whose ready availability had always been taken for granted (except during World War II rationing). The seventies closed with the seizure of American embassy personnel in Teheran and a botched rescue attempt in which much of American troops' military equipment broke down.

It would be surprising if such a string of errors, disappointments, and frustrations had no impact on citizens' confidence. We would expect so many dispiriting events to discourage many regular forms of civic participation. But we would also expect that a fairly rapid return to "normalcy" would leave civic life largely untouched—and permit socioeconomic forces to work their way. We are far from problem-free today, but then when were we? The point is that the extreme buffeting the American social and political system took in the 1970s has largely ended.

Voluntarism and other facets of civic engagement are shaped by three separate sets of factors: (1) core moral commitments, such as understandings of individual responsibility; (2) stages of socioeconomic development, which determine relevant resources; and (3) short-term forces that variously encourage or dispirit the population. There is no indication that the first of these has moved much from its historic course. The second apparently has; the postindustrial setting provides greater resources for engagement by ordinary citizens. The third factor would be expected to produce ups and downs *within* the structure shaped by the first two. Some decline in the 1970s in citizens' confidence and levels of community participation—though hardly a collapse of civic America—would be a likely outcome of the decade's many wrong turns.

A recent study of America's experience with civic participation between 1840 and 1940 gives us further indication of the continuing interaction of long- and short-term forces. Using city directories as a database, Gerald Gamm and Robert Putnam show that "associational density"—the number of associations per 1,000 population—increased sharply over the latter half of the nineteenth and into the early twentieth century, from 2.1 per 1,000 population in 1840 to 5.4 in 1910. The cultural predispositions were present, and urbanization/industrialization dramatically expanded the resource base for group activity.[6] In the next three decades, however, associational density declined from its 1910 high, though it remained well above what it had been in most of the nineteenth century. National traumas, from World War I to the Great Depression, presumably depressed rates of joining, though they didn't alter either the civic culture or the socioeconomic structure. Gamm and Putnam's study stops at 1940, but other data suggest that "associational density" and other civic engagement increased again following World War II, slipped in the 1970s, and rose again after 1980.

CHARITABLE GIVING ON THE RISE

Al and Tipper Gore made headlines when they released their 1997 IRS filing, which showed they had made charitable contributions of just $353. Little wonder many Americans looked askance: Most of them earn far less than the vice president and his wife but give more. An Opinion Dynamics poll for Fox News in April 1998 found only 36 percent reporting gifts to charities that totaled $353 or less. Fifty percent with family incomes in the $25,000-to-$50,000 range said they gave more than the veep did, only 40 percent the same or less.

Individual philanthropy need not involve the face-to-face interaction that comes with participation in community groups, but it reflects an assumption of responsibility for the common good that is part of the idea of social capital. Here the news is astonishingly good. Figure 4.9 shows that Americans are giving much more for philanthropic purposes now than ever before. The best efforts at calculating total charitable giving by individuals (as opposed to foundations, corporations, etc.) pegged the amount at about $10 billion in 1960; thirty-six years later the figure had climbed to $150 billion. Inflation accounts for a part of this gain, of course. But when giving is converted to constant purchasing power (here, what the dollar would buy at its 1993 level) we see that total giving in real terms nearly tripled between 1960 and 1995. Real per capita giving essentially doubled in this span.

The five surveys taken by Gallup for Independent Sector since 1987 all show about 70 percent of U.S. households making contributions each year. These studies estimate that average per-household giving among the seven in ten who gave at about $1,000 in 1995 (Figure 4.10). A survey taken in 1997 by the University of Connecticut's Institute for Social Inquiry found three respondents in every five saying that the amount of money they had contributed over the past two years had held constant; but among those reporting a change in the amount, three in four had increased their giving.

General Social Survey data show similar rates of charitable giving. The 1996 GSS found that three-quarters of the adult population had donated to at least one cause, and one-quarter to three or

Figure 4.9   Charitable Giving Has Been Rising Steadily

	Total Giving (in billions/current dollars)	Per Capita (current dollars)	Total giving (in constant 1993 dollars)	Per Capita (constant 1993 dollars)
1930	$1.2	$10	$10.4	$88
1940	$1.4	$11	$14.4	$112
1950	$4.5	$30	$27.0	$179
1960	$10.4	$58	$50.7	$280
1970	$19.2	$94	$71.4	$349
1980	$48.6	$213	$85.5	$376
1990	$111.9	$448	$124.2	$496
1996	$150.7	$568	$138.9	$524

Source: 1930–1990: U.S. Bureau of the Census, *Statistical Abstract of the United States*, 1995–96, p. 396; idem, *Historical Statistics of the United States, Colonial Times to 1970*, p. 359. 1996: National Report of the American Association of Fund Raising Counsel/Trust for Philanthropy. Constant dollar figures based on calculations from CPI data provided by the Bureau of Labor Statistics.

more (Table 4.2). Both the GSS and the 1995 Gallup survey for Independent Sector show a strong correlation between respondents' incomes and their rates and amounts of giving. But more striking than this iteration that low-income people are less likely than those with high incomes to make charitable contributions is the finding that about *50 percent of respondents with annual incomes under $20,000 were contributors, despite their modest means.* Table 4.3 shows that more low-income contributors made gifts that put some financial strain on them than did wealthier persons. We see this in the giving of various social groups. Combining responses from all five Independent Sector surveys reported from 1988 to 1996, we find that 48 percent of whites with incomes in the $10,000 to $20,000 range reported annual giving of $250 and more to charity, compared to 75 percent of those with $50,000 plus incomes. The same relationships can be seen for African Americans: more giving by those with higher incomes, *but not greater rates of giving compared to income.*

A third of respondents who attended church regularly reported in the 1996 GSS study that they had contributed to three or more organizations or causes, while only 13 percent had given to none.

Figure 4.10   About Three-Quarters of Americans Give to Charities Each Year

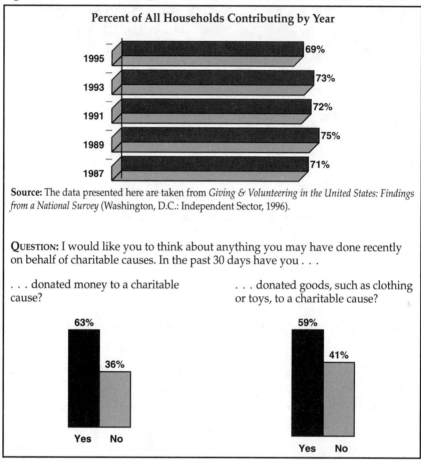

Percent of All Households Contributing by Year

- 1995 — 69%
- 1993 — 73%
- 1991 — 72%
- 1989 — 75%
- 1987 — 71%

Source: The data presented here are taken from *Giving & Volunteering in the United States: Findings from a National Survey* (Washington, D.C.: Independent Sector, 1996).

QUESTION: I would like you to think about anything you may have done recently on behalf of charitable causes. In the past 30 days have you . . .

. . . donated money to a charitable cause?

- Yes 63%
- No 36%

. . . donated goods, such as clothing or toys, to a charitable cause?

- Yes 59%
- No 41%

Source: Survey by the Gallup Organization for CNN/*USA Today*, November 6–9, 1997.

In sharp contrast, over 40 percent who never attended religious services said they made no charitable contributions, and only 13 percent that they had given to three or more causes. The strength of the association between church attendance and charitable giving isn't weakened when one controls for income. For example, half of regular church attendees with low to modest incomes (under $30,000 a year) reported that they had contributed to two or more causes. Only

Table 4.3 Charitable Giving Is Naturally Greater Among Higher Income Groups, But Substantial Among All Groups

By Race and Income:

Percentage Giving:	Whites, by Income				
	Less than $10,000	$10,000 –$20,000	$20,000 –$30,000	$30,000 –$50,000	$50,000+
$250 or less	71%	52%	47%	44%	27%
$250–$1,000	23	32	32	35	34
$1,000–$2,000	5	10	12	11	16
$2,000+	2	6	9	11	22
Percentage Giving:	Blacks, by Income				
	Less than $10,000	$10,000 –$20,000	$20,000 –$30,000	$30,000 –$50,000	$50,000+
$250 or less	79%	68%	67%	44%	24%
$250–$1,000	16	21	21	35	38
$1,000–$2,000	3	8	7	10	19
$2,000+	2	3	4	11	18

Source: Combined surveys by the Gallup Organization for the Independent Sector, 1988, 1990, 1992, 1994, and 1996.

By Income Only:

	Percentage of Respondents Saying They Make Contributions	Average Contributions
Under $10,000	47	$ 295
$10,000–$19,999	51	$ 425
$20,000–$29,999	65	$ 578
$30,000–$39,999	72	$ 722
$40,000–$49,999	75	$ 576
$50,000–$74,999	82	$1170
$75,000-$99,999	80	$1582
$100,000+	89	$3379

Source: Survey by the Gallup Organization for the Independent Sector, 1996.

16 percent in this income bracket who rarely or never attended religious services gave to two or more organizations.

	Number of Organizations/Causes to Which Respondents Contribute			
	None	One	Two	Three or More
Those attending church once a week or more	18%	33%	29%	20%
Those attending church once a year or less	54%	30%	9%	7%

Source: 1996 GSS; respondents with annual incomes under $30,000.

Rates of charitable giving are determined by much more than economic means; they reflect understandings of individual responsibility. In much the same way, as we will see in Chapter 6, differences in rates of giving cross-nationally aren't mere by-products of countries' relative economic standing.

Charitable giving in the United States comes disproportionately from individuals. In 1996, according to data compiled by the AAFRC Trust for Philanthropy and published in its report *Giving USA, 1997*, 80 percent of all philanthropy came through individual giving, as against just 14 percent from foundations and corporations. And, as Figure 4.11 attests, the proportion of Americans supporting religious organizations far surpasses that giving to any other set of groups or causes.

Foundations such as Ford, Rockefeller, Guggenheim, Hewlett, and Packard were established, of course, through individuals' contributions. The U.S. tax code encourages the rich to set up philanthropic foundations by providing that the funds thus contributed pass through without taxation, so long as their subsequent use follows certain rules. The tax code here reflects a national consensus that charitable giving should be encouraged. The creation of private philanthropic foundations is largely an American invention—and we keep creating them in great numbers. The number of newly

Figure 4.11   Where Does Individual Giving Go?

Type of Charity	Percentage of Respondents Giving in Each Area	Average Contribution per Contributing Household
Religious Organizations	48%	$868
Health	27%	$214
Human Services	25%	$271
Youth Development	21%	$137
Education	20%	$318
Environment	12%	$106
Public/Societal Benefit	10%	$122
Arts, Culture, and Humanities	9%	$216
Private/Community	6%	$181
Other	2%	$160
Recreation—Adults	7%	$161
International, Foreign	6%	$283

Source: The data presented here are taken from *Giving & Volunteering in the United States: Findings from a National Survey* (Washington, D.C.: Independent Sector, 1996).

established foundations reached its highest annual rate in the 1980s (a yearly average of 330), and the first half of the 1990s lagged only slightly behind (Figure 4.12). The rate at which new foundations have been set up since 1980 surpasses that for any previous period.

There's been some speculation that the latest crop of superrich Americans (measured now, of course, in billions, rather than millions, of dollars) may be less inclined to engage in philanthropy—the establishment of charitable foundations and the like. In 1997, media mogul Ted Turner joined in this concern and criticism. While announcing plans to donate over a billion dollars to UN humanitarian agencies over the next decade, he challenged other wealthy folk of his generation to do the same. The new computer industry

Figure 4.12   The Number of Foundations Created
Annually Continues to Climb

Foundation "Births" by Decade		
Decade Created	Number	Annual Average
1990–1995	1,495	299
1980–1989	3,304	330
1970–1979	1,047	105
1960–1969	1,740	174
1950–1959	1,935	194
1940–1949	797	80
1920–1939	543	27

Note: The numbers are for foundations with $1 million or more in assets
or making grants (in recent years) of at least $100,000 a year.
Source: *Foundation Giving, 1996,* with an update from the 1997 edition.

billionaires have been a particular target of concern. Are they lagging in terms of philanthropy? In January 1998, Microsoft's Bill Gates fired back in defense that "at age forty-two, I've given at this point a little over five hundred million dollars to foundations that are doing some things I really believe in," and insisted that this was just the beginning of his charitable giving. It would seem sensible to withhold anything like final judgment. Historically, in every period some rich Americans did not give generously to charitable causes, but many who did made their contributions at later stages of their lives. Andrew Carnegie argued that it was fine to accumulate lots of money in one's lifetime—but wrong to die with this wealth still in hand.

Foundation staffs direct their philanthropy to very different groups and causes than do individuals. Data from a sample of about a thousand larger foundations, published in *Foundation Giving, 1996,* show only 2 percent of the awards going to religious organizations or designated for religious purposes. This contrasts to findings of the AAFRC Trust for Philanthropy and Independent Sector that between 40 and 50 percent of individuals' giving goes to the churches. Foundations donate much larger proportions of their awards than do individuals to the arts and humanities, human services, health programs and research, and education.

MUCH MORE THAN WRITING A CHECK

Relatively prosperous individuals find it easy to write checks for good causes; that they do doesn't by itself mean that civic participation is alive and well. If other measures of social capital showed erosion while only check-writing was on the rise, the prognosis for civic America would be gloomy. In fact, though, most measures show participation holding constant or rising. The number of people volunteering their time and services often surpasses those just giving money. The National Commission on Philanthropy and Civic Renewal commissioned the University of Connecticut's Institute for Social Inquiry to conduct a study in which respondents were asked whether they had volunteered or contributed financially to diverse groups and objectives. While the one in five who said he or she had done something recently to help the elderly reported that it was limited to giving money, four in five had given their time (Table 4.4). Even in the case of assisting the poor, two-thirds of those who reported doing something said it was limited to a financial contribution, but the other third worked as volunteers.

"BIOGRAPHY OF A NATION OF JOINERS"

Arthur M. Schlesinger, in a brilliant 1944 essay, wrote that individualism has meant to Americans "not the individual's independence of other individuals, but his and their freedom from government restraint. Traditionally, the people have tended to min-

Table 4.4 It's Not Just Money: In Many Areas, Rates of Volunteering Exceed Those of Giving

QUESTION: There are lots of different causes people volunteer time for and donate money to. For each of the following, please tell me if within the past year you have volunteered time, donated money, or neither volunteered time nor donated money.

Have you volunteered or contributed in order to help . . .

. . . people in need, such as the poor, hungry, or homeless?		. . . youth organizations, like the Boy or Girl Scouts?	
Yes	68%	Yes	48%
Volunteered	24	Volunteered	15
Money only	44	Money only	33
No	32	No	52
. . . religious organizations?		. . . handicapped people?	
Yes	53%	Yes	44%
Volunteered	29	Volunteered	23
Money only	24	Money only	21
No	46	No	56
. . . the elderly?		. . . victims of crime, abuse, or natural disaster?	
Yes	51%	Yes	38%
Volunteered	40	Volunteered	11
Money only	11	Money only	27
No	49	No	61
. . . people who are sick, or working to cure disease?		. . . the environment?	
Yes	50%	Yes	35%
Volunteered	23	Volunteered	14
Money only	11	Money only	21
No	49	No	65
. . . schools, colleges, or other educational institutions?			
Yes	49%		
Volunteered	27		
Money only	22		
No	51		

Source: Survey by the Institute for Social Inquiry, University of Connecticut, for the National Commission on Philanthropy and Civic Renewal, March 14–31, 1997.

imize collective organization as represented by the state while exercising the largest possible liberty in forming their own voluntary organizations."[7] But voluntary action didn't emerge full-blown at the outset; it developed gradually. Voluntarism and other forms of civic engagement were learned skills. "Each fresh application of the associative principle opened the way for further ventures and at the same time helped to provide the needed experience."[8]

Despite a modern-day inclination to romanticize the extent of mutual assistance in the first century or so of the colonial period, the populace showed little understanding of cooperative undertakings, Schlesinger argued. "They had had scant experience in doing things collectively in Europe. Moreover, the population was small, towns were few, and communication was difficult."[9] But with time the reach of voluntarism expanded. Schlesinger thought that the "complete divorce" of church and state was a critical element. Without state aid, "voluntarism . . . became the practice of all devotional associations."[10]

Civic participation evolved so rapidly that by the time of his visit to the United States in 1831–32, Tocqueville could write that "the power of association has reached its uttermost development in America."[11] Technological advances, far from being the enemy of civic engagement, were an essential spur. William E. Channing credited the "immense facility given to intercourse by modern improvements, by increased commerce and travelling, by the post-office, by the steam-boat, and especially by the press. . . . Through these means, men of one mind . . . easily understand one another, and easily act together."[12]

Each stage of socioeconomic development in U.S. history extended resources for civic participation, and experience has established such participation more firmly. Schlesinger saw the progress of associationalism prior to the Civil War as but "a prelude to far greater advances in the years to come. All the earlier favoring conditions now operated with magnified force. Cities were bigger, more numerous, and more generally distributed throughout the land. They were also bound together by swifter

communications. . . . Newspapers not only grew in number and circulation but, themselves obeying the associative impulse, developed chains, syndicated features, and co-operative news-gathering
methods, thereby further increasing the tendency to common
thought and action."[13]

Schlesinger saw the associational impulse expressing itself
ever more forcefully, if at times humorously. "The irrepressible
spirit of gregariousness sometimes [breaks] out . . . in unexpected
forms. Thus the period since the first World War has seen the rise of
the National Horseshoe Pitchers' Association, the Guild of Former
Pipe Organ Pumpers, the Circus Fans' Association of America, the
American Sunbathing Association, and the Association of Department Store Santa Clauses."[14]

The progression of "the associative principle" that Schlesinger
chronicled has continued to our own day, as he expected it would.
He wrote that "out of the loins of religious voluntarism in colonial
times had issued a numerous progeny, each new generation out-
stripping the old in number and variety of its creations."[15] The
postindustrial era is taking this progression to new forms and levels. Civic America continues to reinvent itself.

CHAPTER 5

SOCIAL CONFIDENCE AND TRUST

Contemporary Performance Is Faulted,
but "The System" Is Reaffirmed

By ALL THE BASIC measures—group membership, voluntarism, and philanthropy—civic engagement is as strong today as in times past. Still, there may be underlying trends in citizens' outlook that bode ill for the future. Robert Putnam has argued that Americans are now less trusting of their fellow citizens and society than were their counterparts in the preceding "long civic generation." He observed that "the proportion of Americans saying that most people can be trusted fell by more than a third between 1960, when 58 percent chose that alternative, and 1993, when only 37 percent did."[1] This matters because of the close link between trust and participation. Citing findings of the 1990–93 World Values Surveys, Putnam observed that "across the 35 countries [studied], social trust and civic engagement are strongly correlated; the greater the density of associational membership in a society, the more trusting its citizens." He concluded that *"trust and engagement are two facets of the same underlying factor—social capital."*[2]

He is absolutely correct. Any serious decline of trust in one's fellow citizens, or erosion of confidence in the integrity and moral standing of the social system, are bound in time to corrode citizenship itself. Again, though, we must ask: Are Americans in fact becoming less confident and trusting than earlier generations were? Like other elements of civic engagement, social trust is hard to measure precisely or express in terms of clear trends. One can't imagine a time when all measures were rising or falling together. We must look for the defining pattern.

WIDESPREAD CONCERN

Many contemporary analysts have seen the United States as beset by a crisis of confidence. Such assessments first picked up steam in the early 1970s.[3] Since then, America has often been depicted as a society in decline. Economic decline arguments have been the most common. Historically a "people of plenty," in historian David Potter's words,[4] we were supposedly seeing our economic ascendancy wiped away. In the 1980s Japan's impressive economic achievements were seen making it "Number 1," a condition most Americans found hard to accept.[5] "Red sun rising" hyperbole eventually succumbed to reality, especially following the Tokyo stock exchange crash in 1989. But other threats were quickly discovered.

If the United States was not being overtaken from without, it was perhaps being overtaken from within. A growing income gap between rich and poor was seen challenging Americans' confidence in their society's fairness. Some now argue that the income gap has become the dominant political issue.[6] Throughout his stint as labor secretary in the Clinton administration, Robert Reich repeatedly warned about what he perceived as a "dangerous shift in the distribution of income from ordinary working Americans to the very wealthy." He saw it producing an alarming decline in the public's sense of the system's fairness.[7]

Democratic pollster Stanley Greenberg also sees social trust and cohesion in retreat. Americans believe that people should work hard, take personal responsibility, live by the rules, support their families; and they strive in their own lives to realize these values. Today, though, Greenberg argues, many who hold to these norms "feel that they are not honored . . . and that they are playing by a harder set of rules than others in society."[8] The issue is not, he maintains, "CEOs making more money, it is corporate downsizing and layoffs. It is not about having wealth, it's about having wealth at the expense of people who are working hard. It's not about punitive taxation or redistribution, it is about achieving a society consistent with the norms of working class Americans."[9]

Others see the problem as being quite outside matters of economic conditions. Sociologists James Davison Hunter and Daniel C. Johnson think the American political system may be facing "a legitimacy crisis"—but it's a moral and ethical one, not economic. Citing data from their national survey of "American political culture" taken in the winter and the spring of 1996, Hunter and Johnson argue that "the middle classes on the whole are not especially worried about the national economy, the local economy, about their jobs or their personal finances. Rather, what they fear and what upsets them is the sense that everything they have lived for—their Judeo-Christian God, their family life, their moral commitments, their work ethic, and the public school system that would pass their beliefs on to their children—is in decline and possibly disappearing. *It is not a 'fear of falling' that haunts the middle classes, but a fear of the curtain falling upon their way of life.*"[10]

For yet other observers, the country's low rates of voting give the clearest signal that confidence and trust in the system are eroding. Curtis Gans argues that "the danger to democracy in [high levels of voter abstention] . . . should be self-evident. Because voting is a lowest-common-denominator political act—that is, people who don't vote tend not to participate in any other societally useful activities—decline means both diminution of social capital and a polity increasingly dominated by the self-interested and the zealous."[11] Gans's fascination with alarmist rhetoric is, unfortunately, all too typical of discussions of nonvoting. In fact, no body of available data supports his assertion that people who don't vote don't "participate in any other societally useful activities. . . ."[12]

REASONS FOR CAUTION: ISSUES OF SCOPE AND INTENSITY

Though many are plainly worried, there's reason to be skeptical about the argument that citizen trust and confidence are declining. What's immediately striking is that the argument's proponents mostly ignore *scope and intensity*. Do the familiar trust and confidence questions posed in polls pick up dissatisfactions of limited reach or a withdrawal of confidence deep enough to threaten active citizenship? The distinction is obviously of fundamental importance, but conventional surveys often don't help us make it. To see why, consider this hypothetical exchange between a husband and wife on their tenth wedding anniversary:

SPOUSE 1: Do you know what today is?
SPOUSE 2: Mmmm, no, not offhand.
SPOUSE 1: It's our tenth wedding anniversary, for heaven's sakes!
SPOUSE 2: Oh my gosh! I'm an idiot! I'm sorry I forgot. You're not too angry with me, are you?
SPOUSE 1: Not too angry?! I'm furious! You're the most inconsiderate. . . .

What does this mean? Of course, someone's upset. But the quarrel might be quickly resolved with the performance of minor acts of atonement, leaving a basically healthy marriage unscathed, or it might be "the last straw" in the long deterioration of the marriage, now about to culminate in a breakup. By itself the exchange tells us nothing about the scope and intensity of the spousal conflict, which is really all that matters. We would need to know about many other exchanges, and actual behavior, to tell whether we're dealing with a spat or a crisis.

It's a leap from a family exchange like this one to the broad arena of citizens' trust and confidence in their society and polity, but the analogy is in fact a good one. The 1970s were a rocky decade for the United States, from Vietnam War protests and

Watergate to oil shocks and hyperinflation. Against this backdrop I addressed in a 1976 article the question of how much confidence Americans have in the ability of their society to meet its challenges.[13] The populace could be in a sour mood, angry or bewildered by certain actions, but still retain a high measure of trust in the system's soundness. It was evident that the national mood had been downbeat over the previous decade, but it was harder to determine the depth of the dissatisfaction, and hence its longer-term consequences.

After reviewing the survey data, I concluded that they too often merely confirmed the obvious. "Only a nation of idiots could look at the events of the last decade and say, 'Gee, isn't it all so wonderful!' Of course people are upset. The mere fact of dissatisfaction is scarcely remarkable. How deep is the dissatisfaction?" I found nothing in the data to suggest that the United States was experiencing a legitimacy crisis, or even that it had undergone a loss of confidence in its constituent institutions and processes. "My guess is that the public is saying that the institutions are about as good as human beings are likely to get, but the mix of fools and knaves in the current leadership cohorts has been a bit too rich."[14]

Survey measures show an apparent decline in trust and confidence in aspects of the political system and an increase in public cynicism. When investigators at the University of Michigan's National Election Studies first asked their respondents in 1958 whether they thought "quite a few of the people running the government are a little crooked [or] not very many are, or . . . hardly any of them are . . . ," only 24 percent said "quite a few," while 70 percent said either "not many" (44 percent) or "hardly any" (26 percent). Since then, though, the proportions seeing dishonesty in government have moved up. In three askings of this question by Gallup in 1996 and 1997, just over 50 percent said "quite a few" of those running government are a little crooked, compared with only 45 percent saying "not many" (37 percent) or "hardly any" (8 percent). Similarly, in five national surveys taken by the University of Michigan researchers from 1952 through 1966, not more than

36 percent of respondents (and a low of 25 percent) agreed that "public officials don't care much what people like me think"; the proportion disagreeing averaged in the mid-60s. By the 1990s, however, the Michigan and Gallup surveys were finding that between 55 and 70 percent of respondents agreed that public officials are indifferent to ordinary folks' wishes.

Figure 5.1 brings together a mix of trust-in-government measures. Asked by University of Michigan researchers in 1958 and again in 1964, "How much do you think you can trust the government in Washington to do what is right?," close to three-fourths of respondents chose "just about always" or "most of the time." In six national surveys taken from 1958 through 1972 posing this question, an average of 63 percent expressed trust. But in nine asking between 1974 and 1979, after Watergate and a host of other governmental problems, just 34 percent put themselves in the trusting camp. There was some recovery in the 1980s, when twenty-seven surveys found a 41 percent average saying they trusted the government to do what's right just about always or most of the time; but in forty surveys done since 1990, the average proportion expressing high trust was down again to just 27 percent. A shift over four decades from 63 to 27 percent saying they trusted their national government to do what's right can't be dismissed as inconsequential.

But what do these trends in fact mean, and hence what are their consequences? It's possible that the shifts we've been seeing reflect in part a change in the tone and form of public discourse. We know from candidates' attack ads and televised political shouting matches such as *Crossfire*, that our political "teachers" have been encouraging us to raise the decibel level. Might the proportion of the public inclined in opinion surveys to say "They're crooks" or "I don't trust them" have climbed not so much because of greater dissatisfactions but because political hyperbole has moved center stage?

Still, more than the tone of public discourse is at issue. Many Americans have real concerns with governmental performance. We're troubled by abuses in election finance, by the negative tone of today's campaigns, and by the reach of "special interests" in setting

Figure 5.1   Professed Trust in Federal Government Performance Has Been in a Steep Decline

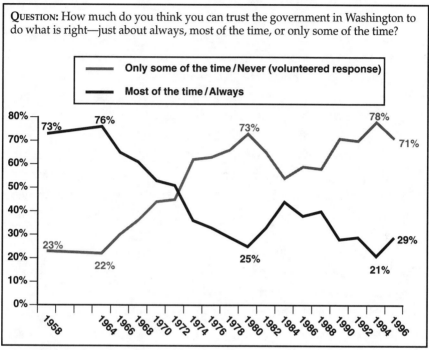

QUESTION: How much do you think you can trust the government in Washington to do what is right—just about always, most of the time, or only some of the time?

Only some of the time / Never (volunteered response)

Most of the time / Always

Source: Surveys by the University of Michigan National Election Studies, latest that of 1996.

public policy. I see a parallel between these contemporary complaints and those early in this century. Large segments of the public during the Progressive Era were frustrated by special interests—"the trusts," corrupt politicians, and political party machines. There was strong support for opening the system up—through direct primaries, referenda, etc.—to take political control away from the interests and "return it to the people." While the Progressive reforms were imperfect and limited in their scope, they accomplished much of what was intended. They reduced public skepticism about the governmental process. From the 1930s through the 1960s, Americans showed little concern about how the game of politics was being conducted. "Process" issues rarely reached beyond political circles, polls show. Since the 1960s, however, public frustrations have been building again. Many now believe that a new set of special interests is wielding excessive control over the political system.

Cyclical ebbs and flows in satisfaction with governmental performance don't tell us much about underlying public confidence or trust. "Trust" must be understood as involving something deeper than calls to public officials to "shape up and do better." Citizens are supposed to holler when things go wrong in the public sphere; and Americans have always had a healthy skepticism about politicians. In 1943, for example, in a poll done by the National Opinion Research Center at the University of Chicago, about half of those surveyed agreed that "it is almost impossible for a man to stay honest if he goes into politics." That's just about the same proportion that Opinion Dynamics found when it asked a similar question in 1997 in a Fox News survey.

Relatedly, since 1945, when Gallup first asked the question, large majorities have said they wouldn't want a son to go into politics as a career. In more recent askings, similarly strong majorities have felt that way about their daughters, too. When Gallup posed a follow-up question about why they didn't want a son to go into politics, most said something about corruption. Americans haven't even been enthusiastic about the prospects of a child of theirs becoming president. If, then, ours is a country where skepticism about politicians has long abounded and a pro-state tradition has been absent, it's hardly surprising that a string of performance abuses would yield a drop-off in "I trust government" answers to survey questions. The latter doesn't tell us that system confidence and support are eroding.

DOES VOTER TURNOUT TELL US MUCH ABOUT POLITICAL SATISFACTION?

The United States' low rates of voting are often cited as a prime indicator of problems in contemporary citizenship. The most widely cited data show turnout down now from its twentieth-

Figure 5.2   The Voter Turnout Story as Commonly Told

Election Year	Percent Who Voted
1960	62.8%
1964	61.9%
1952	61.6%
1968	60.9%
1956	59.3%
1940	58.9%
1936	56.9%
1992	56.2%
1944	56.0%
1972	55.2%
1980	55.1%
1984	54.5%
1976	53.5%
1932	52.5%
1988	51.4%
1948	51.1%
1996	49.0%

Source: U.S. Census data. Calculations are based on census figures for those who voted for president (as the numerator) and voting age population (the denominator) for years listed.

century highs, reached in the 1950s and 1960s (Figure 5.2). These data are compiled by dividing Census Bureau estimates of the *voting age population* into the total of *those who voted for president.* By this accounting, turnout was about 14 percentage points lower in 1996 than in 1960. But Figure 5.2 also reminds us that turnout on the order of 55 percent has been the norm for America since the Great Depression. With lots of elections—local, state, and national; with primaries as well as general elections; and with politics typically conducted in a narrow ideological range where the other side's winning doesn't seem frightening, America's voting rates have long been lower than Europe's. It's an old story, not one of recent shifts in public thinking about government and politics.

Moreover, as political scientist Peter Bruce has pointed out, the widely used turnout figures now significantly overstate nonvoting. Problems occur in both the way numerators (the numbers voting) and denominators (the population base) are calculated. The actual vote is understated because many absentee votes are being left uncounted when turnout numbers are released. This undercount is much greater now than it used to be, owing to "no-excuse-needed" absentee voting on the West Coast, which allows eligible voters to vote by mail for any reason. Bruce shows that "voting by mail injected serious errors into the experts' calculation of West Coast turnouts, since it took up to three weeks in California and Washington . . . to check mail ballots for fraud and then fully report tallies. . . . [V]oting by mail largely accounted for the 2.5 million West Coast votes that were reported *after* the experts made their [turnout] call. . . ."[15]

Far greater exaggeration of nonvoting stems from the practice of dividing the votes cast by census figures on *voting age population* (VAP). The problem is that large proportions of the VAP of the United States—much larger now than in 1960—are by law ineligible to vote because they aren't citizens or because they're convicted felons. Bruce's calculations show that aliens and felons totaled about 17 million people in 1996—8.5 percent of the voting age population—having risen from 10 million and 5.5 percent over the last eight years alone. If the true number casting ballots in November 1996 is divided by the number of *eligible* voters, Bruce calculates, turnout rises to about 54 percent rather than the 49 percent figure widely cited. Thus, turnout in 1996, while lower than the average for the span of elections from the thirties through the nineties, was only marginally so—taking into account the fact that the gap between *voting age population* and *eligible voters* was greater in 1996 than at any time since the big immigration of the late nineteenth and early twentieth centuries.

British political scientist Ivor Crewe has discussed another factor that needs to be considered in evaluating U.S. voter turnout.

He notes that the level of participation in a given election is bound to be influenced by the frequency with which citizens are called to the polls: The more frequent the voting, the less any one contest is apt to stand out. And in this regard, Crewe notes that "no country can approach the United States in the frequency and variety of elections, and thus in the amount of electoral participation to which its citizens have a right. No other country elects its lower house as often as every two years, or its president as frequently as every four years. No other country popularly elects its state governors *and* town mayors; no other has as wide a variety of nonrepresentative offices (judges, sheriffs, attorneys general, city treasurers, and so on) subject to election. Only one other country (Switzerland) can compete in the number and variety of local referendums; only two others (Belgium and Turkey) hold party 'primaries' in most parts of the country. The average American is entitled to do far more electing—probably by a factor of three or four—than the citizen of any other democracy."[16]

I'm not urging complacency about current levels of electoral participation. Voting is a good thing, hardly a demanding task for most of us, and should be encouraged. As Peter Bruce observes, U.S. voter turnout, running between 50 and 55 percent in presidential elections and about 40 percent in off-year congressional contests, "lags far below the turnouts of other Western democracies."[17] But the idea that something dramatic has been happening to turnout levels is wrong, as is the view that current rates signal citizens' malaise.

What's more, if voting rates are down modestly, most other forms of political participation have held steady or climbed. Survey analysis done in the 1960s by Sidney Verba and Norman Nie, and in the 1980s by Verba, Kay Schlozman, and Henry Brady, show the percentage saying they had contacted local, state, or national government officials on political issues much higher in the eighties than in the earlier decade. In fact, of all the areas covered by Verba and his colleagues, only voting in presidential and local elections showed participation declining (Figure 5.3). Similarly, Gallup surveys from the late 1940s through the mid-1960s showed only 7

Figure 5.3   One Leading Study Found Most Forms of Political Participation Up at Least Modestly From the Sixties to the Eighties

	1967	1987	Percentage point change	Proportional change
Contacting Public Officials				
Contact local official: issue-based	14%	24%	10	71
Contact state or national official: issue-based	11%	22%	11	100
Contact local official: particularized	7%	10%	3	43
Contact state or national official: particularized	6%	7%	1	17
Community Problem-Solving				
Work with others on local problem	30%	34%	4	13
Active membership in community problem-solving organization	31%	34%	3	10
Form group to help solve local problem	14%	17%	3	21
Voting and Campaign Activity				
Persuade others how to vote	28%	32%	4	14
Actively work for party or candidate	26%	27%	1	4
Attend political meeting or rally	19%	19%	0	0
Contribute money to party or candidate	13%	23%	10	77
Member of political club	8%	4%	−4	−50
Regular voting in presidential elections	66%	58%	−8	−12
Always vote in local elections	47%	35%	−12	−26

Sources: The 1967 data are reported in Sidney Verba and Norman Nie, *Participation in America: Political Democracy and Social Equality* (New York: Harper & Row, 1972). The 1987 data are from the National Opinion Research Center, General Social Survey.

to 9 percent of respondents having written or wired their members of Congress in the past year. Four studies undertaken in the 1990s, however, have all shown the proportion far higher—in the range of 26 to 31 percent (Figure 5.4). Roper Starch Worldwide regularly asks respondents, as part of its "Roper Reports" polling series, whether they have been participating in a series of political activities—signing petitions, writing their legislators, attending political rallies or speeches, etc. The proportions saying they have been thus engaged show no significant change in these levels of participation over the past two decades (Figure 5.5).

The most commonly cited measures of trust in government report declines. In fact, though, trust levels look very different depending on how the questions are framed. The distinction between government in the abstract, or "Washington," on the one hand, and local government on the other is especially sharp. Surveys taken by Princeton Survey Research Associates in late 1996 and early 1997 for the Pew Research Center found more than three-quarters of respondents nationally and in Philadelphia saying that they felt they could trust their local fire department "a lot" (and another 17 percent, "some"); and nearly half saying that they could trust the police in their area "a lot" (and another third, "some"). Only 6 to 8 percent expressed "a lot" of trust in the national government, and about 40 percent, "some" trust (Figure 5.6).

The PSRA surveys also found that, though aspects of current government performance are criticized, even strongly so, there's a lively sense of citizen efficacy. Only 8 percent interviewed nationally and 6 percent in Philadelphia said they thought that people like themselves can have no impact in making their communities better places to live; another quarter (24 percent nationally, 22 percent in Philadelphia) thought they could have only a small impact. But about 70 percent nationally and in Philadelphia believed they could have a moderate to strong effect on community life—26 percent saying a "big impact" nationally and 29 percent in Philadelphia. These numbers hardly signify a dispirited public feeling estranged from public life. We are unhappy about politicians' behavior and in gen-

Figure 5.4   And Various Surveys Show That the Proportions of the
Public Writing Their Members of Congress Has Increased Over the
Last Half-Century

QUESTIONS: Have you written or wired your congressman during this session of
Congress—that is, since last January 5 [1947]? (Gallup); Have you happened to
write to your congressman during the last year? (Gallup, 1957); During the last 12
months . . . have you . . . written to a U.S. congressman or senator? (Gallup, 1961);
Have you written to your congressman during the last 12 months? (Gallup, 1965);
In the last year, have you . . . written or spoken to an elected representative or
public official, or not? (Harris, 1993, 1994); Have you . . . in the past twelve
months . . . written your congressman or state representative? (ISI, 1994); Have
you written or called a member of Congress in the last year? (Maryland, 1995).

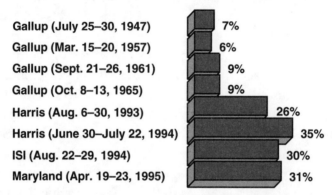

Gallup (July 25–30, 1947)	7%
Gallup (Mar. 15–20, 1957)	6%
Gallup (Sept. 21–26, 1961)	9%
Gallup (Oct. 8–13, 1965)	9%
Harris (Aug. 6–30, 1993)	26%
Harris (June 30–July 22, 1994)	35%
ISI (Aug. 22–29, 1994)	30%
Maryland (Apr. 19–23, 1995)	31%

Sources: Surveys by the Gallup Organization (Gallup), 1947, 1957, 1961, 1965; Louis
Harris and Associates (Harris) for the Henry J. Kaiser Family Foundation and the
Comonwealth Fund, 1993, for Privacy and American Business, 1994; Institute for Social
Inquiry (ISI) for the *Reader's Digest*, 1994; and the Program of International Policy Atti-
tudes, University of Maryland (Maryland), 1995.

QUESTIONS: Have you ever written or wired your congressman or senator in Washington? (Gallup 1946, 1950); Have you ever contacted or written to some representative outside of the city/community? (Harris, 1977); Have you ever written a letter,
sent a telegram, or telephoned the president or a member of congress? (MOR, 1988).

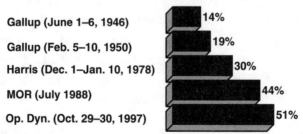

Gallup (June 1–6, 1946)	14%
Gallup (Feb. 5–10, 1950)	19%
Harris (Dec. 1–Jan. 10, 1978)	30%
MOR (July 1988)	44%
Op. Dyn. (Oct. 29–30, 1997)	51%

Sources: Surveys by the Gallup Organization (Gallup), 1946, 1950; Louis Harris and
Associates (Harris) for the U.S. Dept. of Housing and Urban Development, 1978; Market
Opinion Research (MOR) for Rockwell International, 1988; and Opinion Dynamics for
Fox News, October 29–30, 1997.

Figure 5.5   But Another Survey Organization Has Found Levels of
Citizens' Involvement in Politics Unchanged Over the Last Two Decades

QUESTION: Now here is a list of things some people do about government or
politics. Have you happened to have done any of those things in the past
year? [If "yes"] Which ones?

	Jan. 1997	Feb./March 1990	Jan. 1981
Signed a petition	30%	37%	31%
Attended a public meeting on town or school affairs	17	17	15
Written or called any politician*	14	14	10
Served on a committee	9	11	8
Attended a political rally or speech	8	8	10
Served as an officer of some club or organization	7	9	9
Written a letter to a newspaper/ magazine or called a live radio or TV show	6	5	4
Been a member of any group for better government	6	4	4
Worked for a political party	5	4	6
Made a speech	4	5	4
Written an article for a magazine or newspaper	3	2	3
Held or run for political office	1	1	1
None of these	56	51	56

*In 1981 and 1990, the response category was "written your congressman or senator."

Sources: Surveys by Roper Starch Worldwide, 1997; and by the Roper Organization, 1990 and

eral about the way the game of politics is played in Washington. But
we are as optimistic as ever about ourselves.

One last body of data bears importantly on the political/govern-
mental side of trust and confidence. Americans favor modest reforms,
such as in campaign finance and on term limits for elected officials. We
don't support major changes in the structure of the political institutions. By overwhelming majorities we describe the country's constitutional system as sound. We want better performance, but few of us
look longingly at any other governmental system (Figure 5.7).

Figure 5.6   Trust in "My Police and Fire Departments" Is High

Question: . . . For each [institution] . . . tell me whether you feel that you can trust them a lot, some, only a little, or not at all . . . ?

	A lot	Some	A little/ Not at all
The fire department in your area			
Respondents nationally	78%	17%	4%
Respondents in Philadelphia Metro area	78%	17%	2%
The police department in your area			
National	46%	32%	20%
Philadelphia	48%	36%	14%
The public schools in your area			
National	32%	39%	22%
Philadelphia	33%	38%	19%
Local television news channels that cover your area			
National	24%	52%	21%
Philadelphia	27%	47%	23%
The local daily newspapers in your area			
National	22%	49%	26%
Philadelphia	19%	48%	27%
Your city or local government			
National	14%	51%	32%
Philadelphia	14%	50%	33%
Your state government			
National	9%	52%	36%
Philadelphia	8%	50%	38%
The federal government in Washington			
National	6%	42%	49%
Philadelphia	8%	44%	46%

Sources: Survey by Princeton Survey Research Associates for the Pew Research Center. The national survey was conducted February 6–9, 1997. The Philadelphia survey was conducted November 13–December 11, 1996.

Figure 5.7   Despite Our Complaints About Performance, We Think the U.S. Has the Best System of Government

QUESTION: Please tell me if you agree or disagree with the statement. . . . Whatever its faults, the United States still has the best system of government in the world?

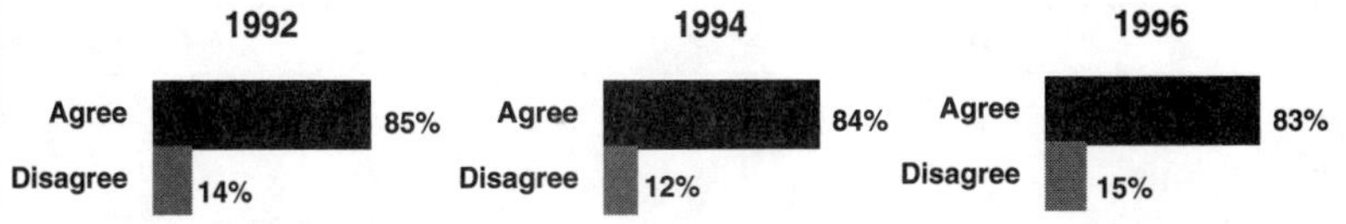

1992	1994	1996
Agree ▓▓▓ 85%	Agree ▓▓▓ 84%	Agree ▓▓▓ 83%
Disagree ▓ 14%	Disagree ▓ 12%	Disagree ▓ 15%

Source: Surveys by ABC News, latest that of May 1996.

THE SOCIETY SIDE OF THE TRUST QUESTION

Issues of social trust and confidence reach well beyond what Americans may think of their country's politics, extending to views of its social system. Is American society a fair one? Does it reward the right values and efforts? Does it extend opportunity to those whose strivings merit it? And are we generally upbeat, or discouraged about the country's prospects?

Asked directly whether they are optimistic or pessimistic about America's future, about seven respondents in every ten have declared themselves optimists in a series of polls taken over the last fifteen years (Table 5.1). Asked "To what extent do you think the best years for America are in the future?," respondents in a 1996 survey by two to one chose "best years ahead" over "no, not ahead." The same two-to-one margin held for most groups in the population—for African Americans as well as whites, women as well as men, low-income manual workers as well as high-income professionals.[18]

Whether citizens see their society giving them a fighting chance to succeed is an important measure of their confidence in it. In a long series of polls reaching back to the early 1950s, Americans by large majorities have said that opportunity is there for average citizens, that "if you work hard you can get ahead—reach

Table 5.1 We're Optimistic About the Country's Future

QUESTIONS: Would you say that you are optimistic or pessimistic about the future of this country? (ABC); In general, are you optimistic or pessimistic about this country's future? (NBC/*WSJ*); Are you optimistic about the future of America? (ORC); [Do you] strongly agree, somewhat agree, somewhat disagree or strongly disagree with the following statement. . . I am optimistic about America's future (Luntz Research Companies).

Date	Organization	Optimistic	Pessimistic
12/83	ABC	73%	21%
9/88	NBC/*WSJ*	77	13
1/92	ORC/MPT	75	23
8/94	Luntz	64	32
5/96	ABC	70	27
11/96	Luntz	67	28

Note: Responses to the Luntz question were combined: strongly/somewhat agree is "optimistic" and somewhat/strongly disagree is "pessimistic."
Source: Surveys by ABC News, NBC News/*Wall Street Journal*, Opinion Research Corp. for Maryland Public Television, and Luntz Research Companies.

the goals you set and more," etc. (Table 5.2). Since the early 1970s, the National Opinion Research Center has been asking its respondents which of two contending propositions accords best with their outlook: "Some people say that people get ahead by their own hard work; others say that lucky breaks or help from other people are more important. Which do you think?" Two-thirds interviewed in 1973 chose getting ahead by one's own efforts, and seven in ten picked that response in 1996.[19] Americans are far more inclined than their counterparts in other industrial democracies to believe that the effort a person makes determines his/her status, rather than that success is more a matter of luck and connections. Roughly two-thirds of U.S. respondents chose the "effort rewarded" end of the continuum in the question posed in the World Values Surveys. In comparison, this answer was picked by only a third or slightly more of respondents in France, Britain, Italy, Sweden, and Japan. Only Canadians evinced the same optimism as Americans on this fundamental dimension of social fairness (Table 5.3).

Table 5.2   We Think Opportunity Is Present, Hard Work Rewarded

QUESTION: Some people say there's not much opportunity in America today—that the average man doesn't have much chance to really get ahead. Others say there's plenty of opportunity, and anyone who works hard can go as far as he wants. How do you feel about this? (1)

	Yes, there's opportunity	No, there's little opportunity
1952	87%	9%

QUESTION: How good a chance do you think a person has to get ahead today, if the person works hard? (2)

	A very good chance	A good chance	Some chance	Little chance	No chance at all
1980	25%	38%	26%	9%	4%

QUESTION: America is the land of opportunity where everyone who works hard can get ahead. (3)

	Strongly agree	Agree	Disagree	Strongly disagree
1980	14%	56%	27%	4%

QUESTION: A basic American belief has been that if you work hard you can get ahead—reach the goals you set and more. Does that still hold true? (4)

	Yes, still true	Not true
1994	74%	24%

QUESTION: Please tell me whether you strongly agree, somewhat agree, somewhat disagree, or strongly disagree with the following statement: "In America, if you work hard, you can be anything you want to be." (5)

	Strongly/somewhat agree	Somewhat/strongly disagree
1994	74%	25%

Sources: 1. Surveys by the University of Michigan National Election Studies, 1952; 2. Surveys by Kluegel and Smith, 1980; 3. Surveys by Kluegel and Smith, 1980; 4. Surveys by the Roper Center for *Reader's Digest*, August 1994; 5. Surveys by Luntz Research Companies, August 1994.

Table 5.3 Does Your Society Reward Effort?

QUESTION: How would you place your views on this scale? 1 means you agree completely with the statement on the left, 10 means you agree completely with the statement on the right, or you can choose any number in between. Left: In the long run, hard work usually brings a better life. Right: Hard work doesn't generally bring success; it's more a matter of luck and connections.

	Scale Responses (*in percent*):		
	Hard work 1–3	4–7	It's more luck 8–10
United States	59	31	9
Canada	55	31	13
West Germany	43	38	14
Britain	38	41	21
France	37	48	13
Italy	35	39	22
Sweden	34	46	18
Japan	33	47	7
Denmark	15	54	31

Source: World Values Surveys, 1990–1993. Those responding "Don't know" are not shown, so percentages sometimes do not add up to 100 (e.g., those of West Germany and Japan).

The United States' competitive position in the world is now widely seen in positive terms, but the prevailing view was far less sanguine in the late 1970s, at various points in the 1980s, and again in the early 1990s. Questions asking how the national economy was performing and how ably or poorly it was being managed often got responses similar to those on governmental performance. But large majorities have consistently said that the American economic system gives people the chance to move ahead. At intervals since 1981, for example, CBS News and the *New York Times* have asked, "Do you think it's possible to start out poor in this country, work hard, and become rich?" Every time, including when the economy was in recession, large majorities have replied affirmatively. Nearly eight in ten did so when the question was last posed (March 1996). Americans distinguish sharply between current performance, where assessments vary depending on conditions, and underlying properties of the country's social, economic, and political institutions. Confidence in the latter has remained high.

Do many CEOs of large corporations cut themselves in on excessive compensation? Many of us think they do. Also true is Stanley Greenberg's assessment that awarding high salaries at the top while downsizing among the troops below breeds resentment. Still, confidence in the fairness of the economic system has remained high. We see this in the unwillingness of large majorities of the population to impose limits on the amount of money an individual is allowed to earn. In a 1994 survey by the Roper Center for Public Opinion Research, conducted for *Reader's Digest*, respondents were asked whether there should be "a top limit on incomes so that no one can earn more than one million dollars a year." Only one in five thought so (Table 5.4). Majorities have given much the same response since polls began posing variants of the question in the late 1930s. Even in 1939, with the Great Depression still hanging over the country, Americans opposed setting top limits on income by two to one and better. Interestingly, the margins against income limits were smallest not at a time of economic privation, but in the middle of World War II. The profound national unity engendered by war-effort sacrifices seemingly gave greater force to the more equalitarian response.

The American ideology has long been distinguished by a far-reaching individualism that inclines many to oppose limits on what people can acquire through their labors. Opposition to income limits reflects this. Even in this context, though, responses to a National Opinion Research Center question in the 1993 General Social Survey are extraordinary. Asked whether they agreed or disagreed that "people should be allowed to accumulate as much wealth as they can *even if some make millions while others live in poverty* [emphasis added]," two-thirds agreed. Such judgments could not survive a widespread sense that the society is unfair.

Americans complain about national shortcomings—as they should. But their general confidence and pride in their society is

Table 5.4 We Say No to Income Limits

QUESTION: Do you think there should be a law limiting the amount of money any individual is allowed to earn in a year?*

	Poll	Yes	No
February 1939	*Fortune*	30%	61%
December 1939	*Fortune*	24	70
March 1940	*Fortune*	24	70
July 1942	*Fortune*	32	60
April 1943	*Fortune*	37	52
June 1946	ORC	32	62
March 1981	Civic Services	20	75
1986	Kluegel/Smith	21	79
January 1992	RSW	9	83
August 1994	Roper Center	22	74

*Question wording varies: February 1939: Do you believe there should be a top limit of income and that anyone getting over that limit should be compelled to turn the excess back to the government as taxes?; July 1942: Question begins "After the war"; April 1943: When the war is over, do you think it would be a good idea or a bad idea for us to have a top limit on the amount of money any one person can get in a year?; June 1946: Do you think it would be a good thing for the country if the government put a top limit on the salary any man could make?; March 1981: Agree/disagree: There should be a top limit on incomes so that no one can earn more than $100,000 a year?; 1986: Agree/disagree: There should be an upper limit on the amount of money any one person can make?; August 1994: Should there be a top limit on incomes so that no one can earn more than one million dollars a year?

Sources: Survey by Elmo Roper for *Fortune*, Opinion Research Corporation, Civic Services, James Kluegel and Eliot Smith, Roper Starch Worldwide, and the Roper Center for Public Opinion Research, University of Connecticut for *Reader's Digest*.

exceptionally strong. That commitment, shown in Table 5.5, is another part of the story of civic America.

THE PERSONAL SIDE OF TRUST

We describe our personal status and prospects in generally positive terms. In the late 1950s Lloyd Free and Hadley Cantril introduced into survey research a measure that they called the "self-anchoring striving scale." Respondents were given a picture of a ladder scale with eleven rungs numbered 0 to 10. The top "represents the best possible life for you as you describe it," the bottom the worst.

Table 5.5 "Proud to be an American" Is Consensual

QUESTION: How proud are you to be an American?

	Very/ Quite Proud	Not Very/ Not at All Proud
June 1981	97%	3%
December 1981	96	3
June 1986	99	1
June 1990	97	2
May 1991	96	3

Source: Surveys by the Gallup Organization, latest that of May 1991.

QUESTION: How proud are you to be an American?

	Poll	Extremely/ Very Proud	Somewhat/ Not Very Proud
January 1989	Michigan	94%	7%
May 1994	NORC	86	14

Source: Surveys by the University of Michigan National Election Studies and the National Opinion Research Center.

QUESTION: How proud are you to be an American citizen?

	Very/Somewhat Proud	Not Very/ Not at All Proud
1995	96	3

Source: Surveys by CBS News, May 1995.

People were then asked where they stood on this "ladder of life" five years earlier, where they are now, and where they expect to be five years hence. The scale has been administered to national samples more than thirty times since 1959.

With only one exception (in 1982) the average placement for "today" averaged higher than that for five years earlier; and in every case respondents on average said they expected to be better off in the future than they were currently. In the first Gallup asking four decades ago, the average placement for five years ago was 5.9, for the present 6.6, and for the future 7.8. In 1996, the last asking to date, the average self-located placements on the ladder of life were

5.8, 6.7, and 7.7 (Figure 5.8). By large majorities, Americans say they are satisfied with the key elements of their status—family, job, standard of living, etc. Eighty-four percent in a February 1997 Gallup survey were content with their jobs. Eighty-five percent had given this same response in 1963 when Gallup first put the question. Eight-five percent expressed satisfaction with their standard of living in 1997; 77 percent had responded similarly a quarter-century earlier. In all cases the proportions expressing satisfaction with the various aspects of their lives and prospects were high, and had either held constant or climbed.

Will America's youth generally do as well as we have? Many people tell survey researchers that they worry about future generations' prospects. But when asked about our own children's prospects, we say in large majorities that we expect our kids' opportunities to be better than ours were. Mothers were asked in 1946 and then again in 1997 whether "your daughter's opportunities to succeed [will] be better or not as good as those you've had." Fathers were asked the same about their sons. The proportion of mothers expecting their daughters' chances to be better than theirs was up sharply (85 percent in 1997, compared with 61 percent in 1946). Fathers weren't as sanguine, but that's probably because they started from higher expectations. Sixty-two percent said in 1997 they thought their sons' opportunities to succeed would exceed theirs, essentially identical to the 64 percent that gave this assessment a half century earlier.

According to two surveys—one national, one in Philadelphia—conducted by Princeton Survey Research Associates in late 1996 and early 1997, Americans by large majorities indicate trust in those with whom they interact closely—in their churches, for example, workplaces, and neighborhoods (Figure 5.9). Sixty-four percent of the Philadelphia respondents, answering another question in this PSRA study, said that "most people can be trusted." Only 25 percent responded, "You can't be too careful in dealing with people." Seventy percent of young people (aged twelve to seventeen) interviewed by Gallup in 1996 agreed with the proposition that "most people are basically good."

Figure 5.8   My Place on the Ladder-of-Life (Better Now Than Five Years Ago; Will Be Better Still in the Future)

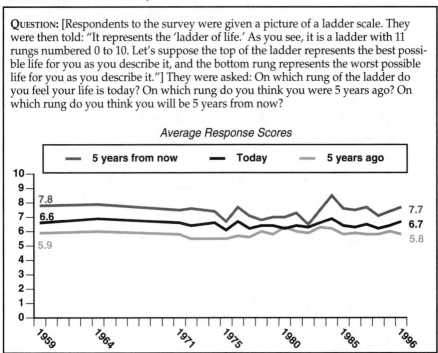

QUESTION: [Respondents to the survey were given a picture of a ladder scale. They were then told: "It represents the 'ladder of life.' As you see, it is a ladder with 11 rungs numbered 0 to 10. Let's suppose the top of the ladder represents the best possible life for you as you describe it, and the bottom rung represents the worst possible life for you as you describe it."] They were asked: On which rung of the ladder do you feel your life is today? On which rung do you think you were 5 years ago? On which rung do you think you will be 5 years from now?

Average Response Scores

Sources: Surveys by the Gallup Organization, 1959–76, 1979, 1981–82, 1985, 1987, and 1989; Cambridge Reports/Research International Incorporated, 1977–78, 1980, 1983–84, 1986, and 1988; and the Pew Research Center, 1996.

EVEN IN THE BIG TROUBLE SPOTS, IT ISN'T TRUE THAT TRUST IS DECLINING

Relations between blacks and whites have long manifested the greatest challenge to social trust in the United States. Yet even here, where conflict is all too prevalent, the trend of the last several decades is positive. By the mid-1990s, when Gallup asked blacks whether they thought only a few whites, many, or almost all white people disliked blacks, 54 percent said such group animus was confined to a few (Figure 5.10). Roper Starch Worldwide found 80 percent of black respondents in a national poll saying that blacks

Figure 5.9   Trust in People with Whom We Live, Work, and Worship Is High

QUESTION: . . . [G]enerally speaking, would you say you can trust [particular group of people] . . . a lot, trust them some, trust them only a little, or not trust them at all?

	A lot	Some	A little/ Not at all
People in your immediate family			
National	84%	11%	4%
Philadelphia	84%	11%	4%
People at your church or place of worship			
National	57%	21%	6%
Philadelphia	59%	22%	4%
Your boss or supervisor*			
National	51%	27%	14%
Philadelphia	51%	27%	14%
People in your neighborhood			
National	45%	36%	16%
Philadelphia	42%	40	15%
People you work with*			
National	41%	40%	17%
Philadelphia	45%	41%	11%
People in the same clubs or activities as you			
National	41%	38%	10%
Philadelphia	42%	38%	8%
People who work in the stores where you shop			
National	30%	50%	17%
Philadelphia	28%	49%	20%

*Based only on those who are employed.
Source: Survey by Princeton Survey Research Associates for the Pew Research Center. The national survey was conducted February 6–9, 1997. The Philadelphia survey was conducted November 13–December 11, 1996.

Figure 5.10   Far Weaker Than We Want, Trust Between Blacks and Whites Is Waxing, Not Waning

QUESTION: In general, how do you think people in the U.S. feel about people of other races? Do you think only a few white people dislike blacks, many dislike blacks, or almost all white people dislike blacks?

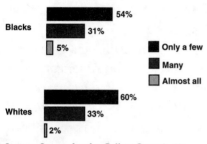

Blacks
54%
31%
5%

■ Only a few
■ Many
☐ Almost all

Whites
60%
33%
2%

Source: Survey by the Gallup Organization, October 5–7, 1995.

QUESTION: From time to time we hear discussions about how well different groups in society get along with each other. I'd like to get your opinion. For each [group] . . . tell me if you think they generally get along very well, fairly well, or not well at all?

... Blacks and Whites

percent responding "Very/fairly well"

Blacks only   80%
All Americans   71%

Source: Survey by Roper Starch Worldwide, Roper Reports 1994–96.

Many Young People in Both Groups Say the System's Fair

QUESTION: Who has a better chance to succeed in life: black people or white people, or do you think they have an equal chance?

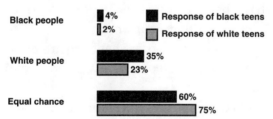

Black people   4%
                    2%

■ Response of black teens
☐ Response of white teens

White people   35%
                    23%

Equal chance   60%
                    75%

Source: Survey by the *Washington Post* of 12- to 17-year-olds in the Washington, D.C., area, December 13, 1995.

and whites generally get along "very well" or "fairly well" (Figure 5.10). In 1981, 54 percent of whites said they knew at least one black person whom they considered "a fairly close personal friend"; by 1997, the proportion was up to 71 percent. African Americans show the same progression. In 1981, 69 percent knew of at least one white person whom they considered a friend, while sixteen years later 83 percent said they did, according to surveys taken by ABC News and the *Washington Post.*

Equally important, despite their strong criticisms of aspects of the country's policies and performance, African Americans now express underlying confidence in the system itself remarkably similar to that of whites. Asked in a *Los Angeles Times* survey of late 1995 whether they believed that "anyone who works hard enough can make it economically" in America, 54 percent of black respondents said that they could and only 30 percent that they couldn't. Among whites, the proportions were 66 percent "can make it," 25 percent "not so." The *Washington Post* asked a sample of black teenagers in the Washington, D.C., area in December 1995, "Who has a better chance to achieve in life—black people or white people, or do . . . they have an equal chance?" Far more (35 percent) said whites have a better chance than said blacks (4 percent), but a large majority (60 percent) said both groups now have equal opportunity.

All sorts of contemporary developments, from high rates of crime and drug use, to family dislocation, to big changes in employment practices, rightly trouble us. Nonetheless, the argument that national confidence and social trust are in retreat simply finds no support in any body of systematic data. Americans express confidence in the institutions of government and economy. We hold firmly to the core values that historically have constituted the United States as a nation. Though many countries around the world are gripped by ideological upheavals, we remain content with our country's long-established social and political ideals.

We still believe opportunity is there for us. What Herbert Croly early in this century called "the promise of American life"—

and what others after him have called "the American dream"—is a promise of real opportunity for individual betterment, if effort is made.[20] Amidst predictions of a closing of the window of opportunity—not so common today, but heard often over the last quarter-century—Americans voiced concerns, but we have continued to see a bright promise in our own lives and in those of our kids.

CHAPTER 6

IN COMPARATIVE
PERSPECTIVE

Two Cheers for American Exceptionalism

THE IDEA OF "American exceptionalism," once widely accepted as a key organizing principle for U.S. social and political experience, has fallen into disfavor. This is unfortunate, because a broad array of data—including some bearing on civic engagement—shows the United States continuing to differ in a patterned way ideologically from countries most like it economically. There are indications that these differences may now be narrowing, but they remain important.

A tour of this topic casts light on issues in the debate about our social health. Can we see trends in civic life around the world? If so, what is driving them? As I will demonstrate, America has always had a richer associational life than most other countries, and that continues today. But there is mounting evidence that civic engagement is increasing globally.

Tocqueville was the first theorist to make the case for American exceptionalism in a systematic fashion. The United States was different from Europe, he argued in *Democracy in America,* because of the way it had experienced the great egalitarian/individualist revolution that was transforming Western societies. Individualist norms, and institutions built upon them, had achieved in this first new nation a triumph unmatched in scope and pace elsewhere.

Tocqueville believed that America's far-reaching individualism accounted for the country's unusually vigorous associational life—though at first glance this result might seem confounding. In fact, individuals who believe they can make a positive difference in society, and that they are morally obligated to try to, are as a consequence more likely to band together with others of like mind. The Reverend William Ellery Channing, a distinguished contemporary of Tocqueville's who met with the great French social theorist in Boston on his U.S. trip, saw individuals gaining strength—enhancing their individuality—through collective action. "Men, it is justly said," Channing wrote in 1829, "can do jointly what they cannot do singly. . . . Men grow efficient by concentrating their powers. Joint effort conquers nature, hews through mountains, rears pyramids, dikes out the ocean. . . . Nor is this all. Men not only accumulate power by union, but gain warmth and earnestness. The heart is kindled."[1] Henry Watterson, another contemporary, argued that "from a handful of individuals we have become a nation of institutions."[2] It usually indicated a sense of strength, not weakness, when an individual sought to "multiply himself" by associations with others.

In Tocqueville's view, America was the great exception because of the way it had experienced the individualist/egalitarian revolution. But he also believed that the revolution would reach out and, eventually, envelop peoples everywhere. It wasn't America's property. His theory envisioned a time when the United States would be less distinctive ideologically than it was in the first half of the nineteenth century.

The country Tocqueville visited in 1831, however, stood out sharply from others. While its democracy was imperfect—flawed most seriously by slavery—the United States was nonetheless the world's only democracy. Its private-property-based economy lacked entirely Europe's feudal and mercantilist traditions. It may have been "self-evident" to Thomas Jefferson and his colleagues when they framed the Declaration of Independence that all people are created equal, endowed by God with unalienable rights to life and liberty and the pursuit of happiness, but such an understanding was emphatically not self-evident to leaders of any other country at the time.

America's comparative position is far less dissimilar today. The ranks of democratic nations have grown markedly since World War II. Countries on every continent have embraced market economies—including countries in Eastern Europe and the former Soviet Union itself that, until a decade ago, championed state socialism. Commitment to expansive notions of individual rights, though far from universal, has become widespread. If we had cross-national public opinion data from Tocqueville's time to compare to what we now have, we would almost certainly see the United States looking far more distinctive ideologically then than now.

THE UNITED STATES IS STILL DIFFERENT

Still, the United States remains ideologically distinctive. Social theorist Seymour Martin Lipset is perhaps the foremost analyst of the origins and implications of the factors in U.S. development that continue to set us apart.[3] Our idea of equality stands out in its emphasis on individual rights. For Americans in all social groups, the goal is extending opportunity, not equalizing results. In a survey the Roper Center did for *Reader's Digest* in August and September 1994, my colleagues and I asked respondents, "Which is more important—insuring that each individual has as much opportunity as possible, even if that means some people enjoy far more success than others, or insuring greater equality of income, even if that limits individual opportunity?" Three-fourths opted for maximum opportunity, however unequal the resulting income distributions might be. Whites were more inclined than African Americans to stress maximizing opportunity, but the latter chose this value over greater income equality by a whopping margin of

65 to 23 percent. Similarly, while high-income people were more likely to say "Extend opportunity," those with annual incomes of less than $20,000 picked it over "equalizing income" by 61 to 24 percent. The survey found no differences at all among age groups.

A number of surveys done cross-nationally—including those taken as part of the International Social Survey Project (ISSP) and the World Values studies—show that Americans still stand out in the extent to which they understand equality in terms of individual opportunity, as opposed to equality of result. Just 39 percent of U.S. respondents agreed that it's government's responsibility to limit income differences—the position of 65 percent of British respondents, 66 percent of West Germans, and 80 percent of Italians (Figure 6.1). Americans were also less likely than citizens of any other of the industrial democracies to agree that "the government should provide everyone with a guaranteed basic income" (Figure 6.1). Similarly, just 23 percent of those in the United States interviewed in 1991 by Times Mirror Center researchers "completely agreed" with the proposition that "it is the responsibility of the government to take care of very poor people who can't take care of themselves." Fully 50 percent of Germans took this stand, as did 62 percent of British and French respondents, 66 percent of Italians, and 70 percent of Russians (Figure 6.2).

When things go wrong, Americans are more inclined to affix responsibility upon the individuals who are involved, rather than on forces beyond individuals' control. Some think the American ideology goes too far in this direction—that those who are seen as unsuccessful are made to bear more blame than they should. That view is prompted, for example, by answers to questions asking about responsibility for poverty, such as one posed on occasion in both Britain and the United States: "In your opinion, which is more often to blame if a person is poor—lack of effort on his part, or circumstances beyond his control?" In 1994, when it was last asked, just 10 percent of British respondents said that the source is most often a lack of individual effort, while 54 percent imputed it to circumstances beyond the control of the poor (Figure 6.3). In the

Figure 6.1   On Equality: Still a Distinctively Individual-Centered Conception

It's government's responsibility to reduce income differences.	It's government's responsibility to provide guaranteed income.

■ Strongly agree   ■ Agree

U.S.	10% / 29%	(39%)
Britain	26% / 39%	(65%)
Canada	16% / 32%	(48%)
Sweden	17% / 36%	(53%)
Italy	40% / 40%	(80%)
W. Germany	20% / 46%	(66%)

U.S.	10% / 24%	(34%)
Britain	27% / 39%	(66%)
Canada	18% / 30%	(48%)
Sweden	10% / 33%	(43%)
Italy	36% / 33%	(69%)
W. Germany	19% / 39%	(58%)

Source: ISSP Surveys, 1992.

United States, however, 44 percent said the problem stemmed from inadequate effort, compared with 34 percent who cited "circumstances." Do you think of your country, British and American respondents were also asked, "as divided into haves and have-nots," or don't you think of it that way? In 1988, the last time the question was asked on both sides of the Atlantic, just one-quarter of Americans but three-quarters of the British saw their country thus severed. American individualism is hardier, more self-confident than its British counterpart.

It naturally follows that Americans are less likely to hold government responsible for seeing to it that everyone is provided for. A question posed in the World Values Surveys, taken in the early 1990s, found 59 percent of U.S. respondents locating themselves on the "individuals are more responsible" end of the continuum, compared with 48 percent of West Germans, 45 percent of the French, 30 per-

Figure 6.2   "It is the responsibility of the state
[in the U.S., "the government"] to take care of very
poor people who can't take care of themselves."

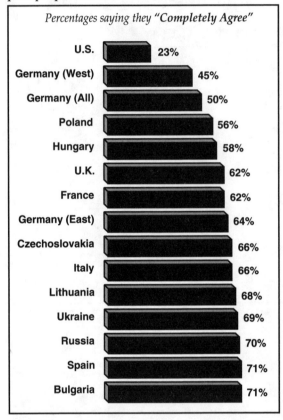

Source: Surveys taken for the Times Mirror Center, spring 1991, for
the countries shown.

Figure 6.3   What's the Prime Cause of Poverty—Lack of Individual
Effort, or Circumstances Beyond One's Control?

QUESTION: In your opinion, which is more often to blame if a person is
poor—lack of effort on his part, or circumstances beyond his control?

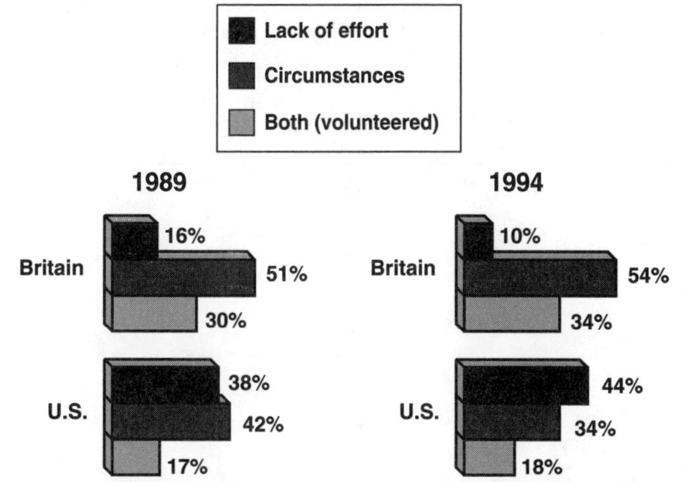

■ **Lack of effort**

■ **Circumstances**

■ **Both (volunteered)**

1989

Britain
16%
51%
30%

U.S.
38%
42%
17%

1994

Britain
10%
54%
34%

U.S.
44%
34%
18%

Sources: Surveys (for Britain) by the British Gallup Organization, 1989 and 1994; and
(for the U.S.) by the Gallup Organization, 1989, and CBS News/*New York Times*, 1994.

cent of the British, 29 percent of Italians, and only 17 percent of the
Japanese (Table 6.1).

RELIGIOUS EXCEPTIONALISM

Churches and other religious bodies play dominant roles in America's associational life and are the principal beneficiaries of individual
philanthropy. Analysts have noted that, religiously, the United States
doesn't behave as it "should," given its economic, technological, scientific, "postindustrial" development. Walter Dean Burnham, a political scientist at the University of Texas, has observed that "the
proposition suggests itself that the higher the level of development in
a given society [meaning here advanced industrialism], the smaller

Table 6.1 Where Does Responsibility Rest—With the Individual or the State?

QUESTION: Now I'd like you to tell me your views on various issues. How would you place your views on this scale? 1 means you agree completely with the statement on the left, 10 means you agree completely with the statement on the right, or you can choose any number in between. (Left = 1) Individuals should take more responsibility for providing for themselves. (Right = 10) The state should take more responsibility to ensure that everyone is provided for.

	Scale Responses		
	1–3	4–7	8–10
France	45	40	13
Britain	30	45	24
West Germany	48	34	15
Italy	29	39	28
Denmark	43	47	11
Canada	50	35	14
Japan	17	41	37
Sweden	62	30	6
United States	59	31	9

Source: World Values surveys, 1990–1993.

will be the fraction of its population for whom religious beliefs are of great importance."[4] Burnham tested this proposition by locating a large number of countries on two measures: the extent of their economic development, and the extent to which their citizens see religious beliefs as important in their lives. "Two things are immediately visible on inspection," Burnham wrote. "First, the overall relationship is not only positive, it is nearly linear and extremely strong." In general, the more developed the country, the lower the importance citizens attach to religion. But this is emphatically not true in the United States, which is highly developed *and* very religious.

Americans differ greatly from their counterparts in Europe's industrial democracies in church attendance, the strength of professed religious attachments, and adherence to traditional religious beliefs (Figure 6.4). Peter F. Drucker has described "the peculiarly American symbiosis of secular state and religious society," which he calls "the cornerstone of the American commonwealth." He sees the

Figure 6.4   Religiosity: The United States Is Still the Great Exception

	U.S.	Sweden	France	W. Germany	Britain	Spain
1. ". . . would you say you are . . ."						
A religious person	82	29	48	54	55	64
Not a religious person	15	56	36	27	37	27
A convinced atheist	1	7	11	2	4	4
Don't know	2	9	5	17	4	5
2. ". . . Life is meaningful only because God exists . . ."						
Agree	59	14	27	25	35	33
Disagree	31	73	56	49	52	46
Neither	7	7	12	9	8	16
Don't know	3	7	5	17	5	4
3. ". . . about how often do you attend religious services . . ."						
Once a week or more	44	4	10	18	14	29
4. Percent saying they believe in heaven						
	84	26	27	31	57	50
5. Percent saying they believe in hell						
	67	10	15	14	27	34
6. "I never doubt the existence of God."						
Completely agree	60	NA	29	20	31	54

Note: Responses are in percentages.

Sources: Questions 1–3 are for the World Values Survey, 1990–1993. This survey was done by the World Values Study Group, part of the Inter-University Consortium for Political and Social Research. The samples consist of adults age 18 and over, in 45 countries. The in-person interviews were conducted by local survey organizations. Sample sizes varied from country to country. Questions 4 and 5 are for a cross-national survey done by the Gallup Organization for Applied Research in the Apostolate, 1981; question 6 is from cross-national surveys done for the Times Mirror Company.

United States as in one sense both the "oldest and most thorough-going secular state." But it is also "the only society in the West in which belief in a supernatural God is taken for granted and in which the traditional religious bodies, the churches, continue to discharge, unchallenged, many important community functions. . . . Everywhere else the secular state arose out of a revolt against religion. In this country the secular state owes its existence largely to the demand of the leaders of dominant, indeed of established, religious creeds that civil power and religious society be strictly separated for the greater good of religion and church."[5]

S. M. Lipset notes that a number of observers have traced America's extensive voluntarism, so supportive of its political democracy, to the phenomenon of "voluntary religion." Lipset himself argues that "the end of religious Establishment and the growth of the sects meant that a new structure of moral authority had to be created to replace the once dominant link between Church and State. In New England, many Congregationalist ministers and laymen consciously recognized that they had to establish voluntary organizations to safeguard morality in a democratic society that de-emphasized the links between Church and Government. The early organization of local and national associations for domestic missionary work, for the distribution of Bibles, for temperance, for opposition to slavery . . . was invariably undertaken by [those] who felt these were the only ways they could preserve and extend a moral society. Eventually a host of voluntary groups developed around the voluntary churches."[6] Calvin Colton reached this same conclusion in the 1830s:

> The separation of Church and State, and other causes, have given rise to a new species of social organization, before unknown in history. . . . Then opened on the American world the new era of the Religious and Benevolent Society system, and summoned into the field an immense body of superior and highly-cultivated talent. . . . As to the right or wrong of these institutions, or as to

whether they are good or bad, is not, in this place, a subject of inquiry: but simply the fact of their social importance, and their power. . . . And it happens, that these voluntary associations are so numerous, so great, so active and influential, that, as a whole, they now constitute the great school of public education, in the formation of those practical opinions, religious, social, and political, which lead the public mind and govern the country. . . .[7]

THE UNITED STATES AND OTHERS COMPARED ON GROUP PARTICIPATION, VOLUNTARISM, AND PHILANTHROPY

Americans' responses on matters of civic engagement are a direct by-product of their ideology; they are a primary expression of the country's pervasive individualism. And however much movement there's been since Tocqueville's day—and in the last quarter-century in particular—toward lessening America's historic ideological exceptionalism, we remain distinctive. It isn't surprising, then, that we continue to stand out in rates of civic engagement. Drucker calls voluntary group action "that peculiarly American form of behavior." He argues that "nothing sets this country as much apart from the rest of the Western World as its almost instinctive reliance on voluntary, and often spontaneous, group action for the most important social purposes."[8] A growing body of empirical data supports this assertion, and its application to the contemporary scene, not just to the past.

Until recently, systematic cross-national data on group participation and voluntarism were as scarce as hens' teeth. Even now, set against the enormous amount of other social and economic data collected, it is in remarkably short supply. Lester Salamon and

Helmut Anheier note that "despite its importance, the nonprofit, or civil society, sector has remained an uncharted subcontinent on the social landscape. One reason for this is doubtless empirical. The data systems used to gather information about the structure of economic life have systematically overlooked this sector or essentially defined it away."[9]

This oversight is finally being remedied. The World Values surveys, conducted in many countries between 1990 and 1993, gave respondents lists of voluntary groups and private associations and asked them which, if any, they belonged to. Only 18 percent of Americans said they belonged to none, compared with 33 percent of West Germans, 35 percent of Canadians, 61 percent of the French, and 64 percent of Japanese (Figure 6.5). At the other end of the continuum, 19 percent of Americans belonged to four or more groups, as against 4 percent of Italians and 4 percent of the French. Of all the countries covered in these surveys, only the Netherlands rivaled the United States in frequency of group memberships: just 15 percent of Netherlands respondents reported belonging to no group—actually lower than the 18 percent so reporting in the United States, though the difference isn't meaningful statistically. America leads all countries in the proportion of its population belonging to religious organizations, while the Netherlands leads everyone in membership in environmental, educational, and cultural groups (Figure 6.6). A follow-up series of World Values surveys taken between 1995 and 1997 shows this same U.S. distinctiveness (Figure 6.7).

America's ethic of personal responsibility is typically not the harsh individualism portrayed by critics. We may be less inclined than other peoples to rely on governmental efforts on behalf of the needy, but we are far more inclined to back private efforts and to stress our common individual responsibility. Virginia Hodgkinson, vice president for research at Independent Sector, writes that Americans believe that individuals have the responsibility "to help others in need and to improve the quality of their communities. In the 1988 Independent Sector survey, 75 percent agreed that it is the responsibility of individuals to give what they can to charity." She

Figure 6.5   Americans Stand Out as "Joiners"

	Percent belonging to at least 1 group	Percent belonging to no groups
U.S.	82%	18%
Netherlands	85%	15%
W. Germany	67%	33%
Canada	65%	35%
Britain	54%	46%
Italy	41%	59%
France	39%	61%
Mexico	36%	64%
Japan	36%	64%
Spain	30%	70%

Source: World Values Survey, 1990–1993.

Figure 6.6 Americans Stand Out Most in Religious Group Participation

Percentage Claiming Membership, by Type of Association

QUESTION: . . . Which, if any [of these groups], do you belong to?

	U.S.	Netherlands	Canada	Mexico	France
Religious organizations	47%	35%	25%	14%	6%
Education/cultural groups	20	35	18	12	9
Professional associations	15	13	16	3	5
Youth work groups	12	7	10	4	3
Social welfare groups	9	15	8	5	7
Environmental groups	8	24	8	3	2
Women's groups	8	6	7	2	1

	Britain	W. Germany	Italy	Spain	Japan
Religious organizations	16%	16%	10%	5%	7%
Education/cultural groups	10	12	7	5	6
Professional associations	11	9	6	3	4
Youth work groups	4	4	4	2	*
Social welfare groups	7	7	5	3	1
Environmental groups	6	5	5	1	1
Women's groups	5	6	*	1	3

*Less than 1%

Source: World Values Survey, 1990–1993.

Figure 6.7   Americans Still Distinguished as Joiners

QUESTION: Now I'm going to read off a list of voluntary organizations. For each one, could you tell me whether you are an active member, or inactive member, or not a member of that type of organization?

*Percentage of the public who participate **actively***

	Church or religious organization	Sport or recreation	Art, music, or educational organization	Professional organization
Argentina	15%	8 %	10%	5%
Brazil	31	13	11	10
Germany				
Western States	16	35	12	5
Eastern States	8	21	9	4
Japan	5	12	6	7
Mexico	39	24	21	11
Norway	8	23	15	9
Spain	17	13	8	4
United States	51	24	22	21

	Charitable organization	Environmental group	Political party	Union
Argentina	6%	3%	3%	2%
Brazil	15	6	7	10
Germany				
Western States	8	3	4	6
Eastern States	7	1	3	8
Japan	1	1	2	3
Mexico	9	9	9	10
Norway	9	1	3	16
Spain	5	3	2	3
United States	26	9	20	10

Source: World Values Survey, 1995–97.

Note: Some major countries for which we wish data were available—such as Great Britain and Italy—were not covered in this round of World Values research.

contrasted this response to that given to the same question in Great Britain in the 1988 *Charity Household Survey:* Only 46 percent thought that individuals had the responsibility to give what they could. And while this or comparable questions haven't been asked in broader cross-national surveys of giving, Hodgkinson notes that "other available data suggest that many in Western Europe and in Canada rely on strong government intervention to assist people in need. In the United States, most believe that helping others is an individual obligation as well as the responsibility of government."[10]

For nearly a decade now, the Johns Hopkins Comparative Nonprofit Sector Project has conducted surveys of giving and volunteering in Western Europe, modeled after those done in the United States by Gallup for Independent Sector. Surveys taken in Germany and France in 1991 found just 13 and 19 percent, respectively, saying they had volunteered their services for civic activities in the preceding year, compared with 49 percent so reporting in the Independent Sector study done at about the same time. Similarly, whereas 43 percent of French respondents and 44 percent of Germans had made financial contributions in the previous twelve months, 73 percent of Americans reported having done so (Figure 6.8). Anheier and his colleagues noted too that "the average sum of money donated . . . amounted to $851 in the US, $120 in Germany, and $96 in France. . . . [T]he average US contribution outweighs the French and German ones seven or eight fold."[11] Americans donated about 1.2 percent of their annual incomes in 1991—a proportion that has remained constant. In contrast, Germans donated just 0.3 percent of their income and the French just 0.15 of theirs.

As in other comparative survey research, the Johns Hopkins studies found "the religion factor" shaping a major difference between U.S. and Western European giving patterns. The absence of a state church benefiting from tax support sets America apart. In Germany, both the Catholic and Lutheran churches receive billions of marks annually from government-imposed church taxes. Citizens decide which church will get their "contribution," but

Figure 6.8   Volunteering and Giving: Again the U.S. Is Different

	U.S.	Germany	France
Percent of respondents who volunteered during previous 12 months	49%	13%	19%
Percent of respondents who contributed during previous 12 months	73	44	43
Average sum of donations for previous 12 months for givers	$851	$120	$96

Sources: Survey by the Gallup Organization (U.S.) for the Independent Sector, latest that of 1991; Zentrum für Umfragen, Methoden und Analysen & Gesellschaft für Marketing-Kommunikations-und Sozialforschung mbH (Germany), 1992; and I.L.S. Survey for Laboratoire D'Économie Sociale and the Fondation de France (France), 1991.

they can't decide not to pay it. Excluding these funds, only about one-quarter of Germans in the Johns Hopkins studies made church contributions; the proportion was even lower—9 percent—in France. In contrast, the 1991 Gallup survey for Independent Sector found 51 percent of U.S. respondents saying they had made contributions to religious groups in the previous year. And the gap between the proportion of Americans volunteering their time for church-related community activities as compared with their German and French counterparts was even wider (Figure 6.9).

The Johns Hopkins research finds comparable patterns in each country in the rates at which various social groups contribute and volunteer. In the three countries covered by the 1991 surveys, for example, frequent church attendees were more likely to give and volunteer than nonattendees, and those with high socioeconomic status more likely than those of lower status (Figure 6.10).

Lester Salamon, Helmut Anheier, and their colleagues completed a major study in 1996 of the scope, organizational structure, financial base, and role of the "nonprofit sector" in a broad selection of countries from North America and Western Europe, plus Egypt, Thailand, India, and Japan. They focused on what they called the

Figure 6.9   Proportions of the Public Giving and Volunteering, by Sector

	Giving			Volunteering		
Sector	U.S.	Germany	France	U.S.	Germany	France
Culture & Recreation	16%	9%	2%	13%	6%	9%
Education & Research	21	2	8	15	1	2
Health	33	13	23	13	1	2
Social Services	50	13	10	27	1	3
Environment	16	9	2	9	1	1
Advocacy	12	3	2	5	2	1
Philanthropy	16	1	1	9	*	*
International	4	15	7	2	*	1
Professional	16	2	2	7	1	1
Religious w/o church tax	51	24	9	27	3	2
Religious w/church tax	NA	Over 90%	NA	NA	NA	NA
Other	3	3	1	3	1	1

*Less than 0.5%

Sources: Survey by the Gallup Organization (U.S.) for the Independent Sector, latest that of 1991; Zentrum für Umfragen, Methoden und Analysen & Gesellschaft für Marketing-Kommunikations-und Sozialforschung mbH (Germany), 1992; and I.L.S. Survey for Laboratoire D'Économie Sociale and the Fondation de France (France), 1991.

Figure 6.10   The Demography of Public Giving and Volunteering

	Giving			Volunteering		
	U.S.	Germany	France	U.S.	Germany	France
Sex						
Male	70%	40%	39%	53%	16%	21%
Female	74	50	46	47	11	18
Religion						
Protestant	74	44	56	51	12	6
Catholic	76	49	48	48	12	21
Other/None	64	39	34	42	19	17
Church Attendance						
Frequent	84	58	62	62	18	27
Less frequent	63	43	47	37	10	20
Rarely/Never	57	29	40	31	14	17
Occupation						
Professional	86	66	49	70	18	28
Self-employed	85	47	48	59	19	27
White collar	77	42	47	58	15	23
Blue collar	66	39	21	45	15	15
Not employed	68	50	50	38	10	15
Education						
Primary	48	47	39	20	9	11
Secondary	73	46	44	46	16	21
Advanced	84	41	53	67	21	30

Sources: Survey by the Gallup Organization (U.S.) for the Independent Sector, latest that of 1991; Zentrum für Umfragen, Methoden und Analysen & Gesellschaft für Marketing-Kommunikations-und Sozialforschung mbH (Germany), 1992; and I.L.S. Survey for Laboratoire D'Économie Sociale and the Fondation de France (France), 1991.

"key institutional component of civil society: private voluntary, or nonprofit, sector, which we define as a set of entities that is (1) organized, (2) private, (3) non-profit-distributing, (4) self-governing, and (5) voluntary to some meaningful extent."[12] They didn't examine groups involved in religious life or individuals' participation outside of formal organizational settings. The Hopkins investigators found that the civil society sector is now a major force in most of the countries they examined, its presence far more widespread than is typically thought.

> ... [T]he number of associations has increased substantially in recent years. In France, over 60,000 associations were created in 1990 alone, compared to less than 18,000 in 1961. Similarly, in Germany, the number of associations per 100,000 population nearly tripled from 160 in 1960 to 475 in 1990. Even Hungary, within two years of the fall of communist rule, boasted over 13,000 associations. And Sweden, often regarded as the prototypical welfare state, displays some of the highest participation rates in civil society worldwide: Most Swedes belong to one or more of the country's close to 200,000 membership associations, creating a dense social network of 2,300 associations per 100,000 population.[13]

Salamon and Anheier sum up their research findings as showing a "'global associational revolution' of extraordinary scope and dimensions."

Nonetheless, the United States continues to stand out in the reach of its nonprofit sector. We not only have more voluntary, not-for-pay civic activity than other countries, but also more private, not-for-profit organizations. The IRS's master list of nonprofits (tax-exempt organizations) reached over 1.1 million in 1994, up by 200,000 from seven years earlier (Figure 6.11). According to the Johns Hopkins research, American nonprofits spent nearly $350 billion in 1990, or 6.3 percent of GDP. British nonprofits ranked

Figure 6.11   Associational America: The Nonprofits Continue
to Proliferate

Type of Tax-Exempt Organization	Active, 1987	Active, 1994
Religious, Charitable, etc.	422,103	599,745
Social Welfare	138,485	140,143
Fraternal Beneficiary Societies	98,979	92,284
Business Leagues	59,981	74,273
Labor, Agricultural Organizations	75,238	68,144
Social and Recreational Clubs	60,146	65,273
War Veterans' Organizations	24,749	30,282
Credit Unions	6,652	5,391
All Others Combined	52,772	63,063
All Tax-Exempts	939,105	1,138,598

Note: Number of active organizations on IRS's master file of the tax-exempt.
Source: *The Nonprofit Almanac* 1992–1993, p. 24; 1996–1997, p. 38 .

closest to the United States, spending 4.8 percent of GDP. Italy, with
a population roughly one-fifth that of the United States, ranked far
below (Figure 6.12). A much higher proportion of Americans than
of other nationals find employment in nonprofit organizations: 6.9
percent of total employment in the United States, compared with
4 percent in the U.K. and 2.5 percent in Japan (Figure 6.13).

In describing the expanding role of nonprofits in countries
with diverse historical traditions and rates of industrial development, Salamon and Anheier reject "the dominant 'market failure/
government failure' theory and the conservative concept of an
inherent conflict between the nonprofit sector and the state that is a
natural corollary of it."[14] They note that influential conservative
analysts like Robert Nisbet have found government "a bureaucratic monolith inherently hostile to alternative centers of power.
As the state expands, it therefore renders voluntary organizations

Figure 6.12   Spending by Nonprofits in the U.S. Surpasses That in
Other Industrial Democracies

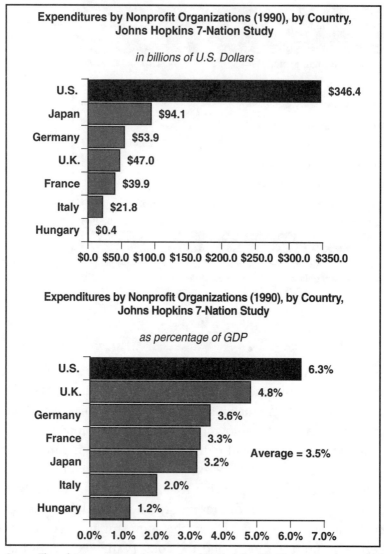

Source: These data were compiled and analyzed for the Johns Hopkins comparative nonprofit sector project. They are reported in Lester Salamon and Helmut K. Anheier, *The Emerging Non-profit Sector* (Manchester, U.K.: Manchester University Press, 1996).

Figure 6.13 So Does Employment in the Nonprofit Sector

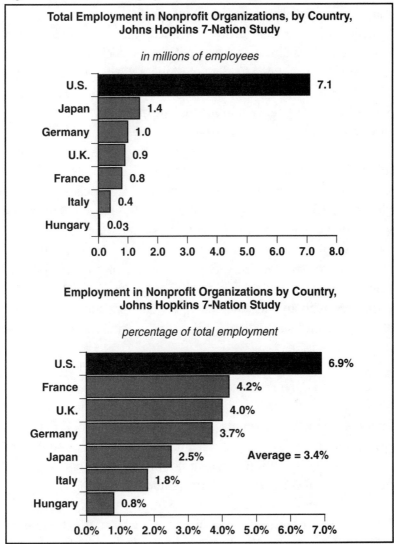

Total Employment in Nonprofit Organizations, by Country, Johns Hopkins 7-Nation Study

in millions of employees

U.S.	7.1
Japan	1.4
Germany	1.0
U.K.	0.9
France	0.8
Italy	0.4
Hungary	0.03

0.0 1.0 2.0 3.0 4.0 5.0 6.0 7.0 8.0

Employment in Nonprofit Organizations by Country, Johns Hopkins 7-Nation Study

percentage of total employment

U.S.	6.9%
France	4.2%
U.K.	4.0%
Germany	3.7%
Japan	2.5%
Italy	1.8%
Hungary	0.8%

Average = 3.4%

0.0% 1.0% 2.0% 3.0% 4.0% 5.0% 6.0% 7.0%

Source: These data were compiled and analyzed for the Johns Hopkins comparative nonprofit sector project. They are reported in Lester Salamon and Helmut K. Anheier, *The Emerging Nonprofit Sector* (Manchester, U.K.: Manchester University Press, 1996).

functionally irrelevant, thereby contributing to their decline and undermining the spirit community which they sustain."[15]

Instead, Salamon and Anheier argue, while there are instances where the state militates against an active civil society sector—with twentieth-century totalitarianism obviously the most thoroughgoing and tragic—"there are at least as many where the relationship is one of interdependence and mutual support. This is clearly evident in the striking record of governmental support for the nonprofit sector. . . . The state has emerged in the modern era not as a displacer of nonprofit activity, but as perhaps the major 'philanthropist,' underwriting nonprofit activity and significantly extending its reach."[16] The authors point out as well, though, contemporary cases in democracies where government's hand among nonprofits is too heavy. They cite in particular Japan, "where nonprofit organizations have been actively enlisted in the provision of state-financed services, but always on terms defined mostly, indeed almost exclusively by the state. The upshot has been to convert nonprofit organizations into mere 'agents' of the state, rather than true 'partners' with it."[17]

Sorting out, for the United States or any other country, instances where government action encourages and vitalizes nonprofits from those where government tends to dominate, turning them into quasi-governmental appendages, is well beyond the reach of my inquiry here. I do agree with Salamon and Anheier that there is no necessary opposition between on the one hand a substantial governmental role in extending services and ministering to community needs and on the other an active civic engagement that is truly independent, self-starting, and voluntaristic. But it must be noted that the vast expansion of the nonprofit sector that the Johns Hopkins investigators have found seems to have resulted in large measure from the spread of individualism around the world, along with increased doubts about reliance on state action.

America continues to stand out as a nation of joiners. This is most dramatically the case with regard to participation at churches and in other religious organizations. Elsewhere, though, the latest global data point to a widespread expansion of associational engagement. In general, the nongovernmental dimension of civic life is growing in many countries. Thus, Tocqueville's prediction that other nations will follow, on their own terms, the course the United States first charted is being borne out.

AFTERWORD

T HE GREATEST ACHIEVEMENTS of the United States are political. This claim may strike some as curious, since rank-and-file Americans have rarely been absorbed in politics. Activities outside the political arena, especially religious and economic pursuits, have typically seemed far more compelling than anything inside it. What's more, Americans have been relatively disinclined, compared with citizens of other democracies, to look to government. Nonetheless, the United States has led the way in three political developments of extraordinary importance.

First, it has innovated ideologically, establishing by the end of the eighteenth century a far-reaching individualism as the core of its social and political commitments. For a long time thereafter, the United States was a lonely outpost of this revolutionary new idea system. Now, in the late twentieth century, however, expansive claims of individual rights are on the rise globally—seen in the advance of political democracy, market economies, and egalitarian social norms. It's no exaggeration to say that much of the world now strains for more individuation and democracy. Individualist ideology isn't any country's property—but its elaboration is a distinctly American contribution.

The second great political innovation came in political institutions. Creation of the system we call "Madisonian"—in which James Madison indeed had the leading role but many others played important parts—successfully institutionalized the ideology. For individuals to be strong politically, Madisonianism posited, government must be carefully *limited*. Not *weak;* it's no great feat to create a weak state. But Madison and his colleagues in the Philadelphia Convention of 1787 wanted a national government strong enough to advance their primary goal of American nation-building, and then energetic enough to defend and maintain the new nation.

The Supreme Court (and federal court system) they created isn't weak; it's the strongest in history. The presidency they established leaves one person holding "the executive power"—commanding the armed forces, making treaties, nominating all federal officials for posts from embassies abroad to the federal bench, vetoing legislative enactments, removing from office unilaterally executive department heads and their subordinates. Similarly, the national legislature the founders established has extraordinary independence and broad powers—witness the breathtaking grant of Article I, Section 8 of the U.S. Constitution. But these strong institutions are pitted against each other, through an elaborate separation of powers and checks and balances. "In framing a government which is to be administered by men over men," Madison wrote in Federalist Paper 51, "the great difficulty lies in this: You must first enable the government to control the governed; and in the next place oblige it to control itself."

America's third major political contribution is the one whose present status I've been assessing here—an unusually expansive and demanding sense of citizenship. In this individualist rendering, the citizen has responsibilities for the health and well-being of his society that extend far beyond his relationship with the state. Voting and other directly governmental forms of participation are important, but they aren't the dominant part of civic involvement. Americans exercise their citizenship in thousands of ways—they join what William Channing and Alexis de Tocqueville called "societies," volunteer for community service, give money to a church, a high school band club, or the United Way.

PERMANENT ANXIETY

Yet if citizenship is one of America's proudest claims, it is at the same time a most demanding ideal. We inevitably fall short of the ideal—and worry about it precisely because it is so important to us. Each generation has evinced concern about the condition of citizenship and whether certain trends are leaving it diminished.

James Bryce began his monumental study of the United States in the late nineteenth century puzzling over why Americans had kept asking him what he thought of their country's institutions: "In England one does not inquire from foreigners, not even from Americans, their views of the English laws and government; nor does the Englishman on the continent find Frenchmen or Germans or Italians anxious to have his judgments on their politics."¹ Bryce concluded that Americans differed in this regard because our institutions are something "invented" rather than "grown." They represent an elaborate, highly self-conscious experiment in nation-building. The American nation isn't based, as most countries are, on a shared ethnicity but rather on a shared political philosophy. Frenchmen, Germans, the English, and others have debates aplenty about what values and programs their nations should pursue, but no one thinks that the existence of France, Germany, or England is predicated upon the strength or validity of any set of answers. America's national existence *was,* and though we're much older and in a sense more established now, still *is.*

The vitality of the answers defining our nationhood depends almost entirely upon ordinary citizens. No one understood this better than the English philosopher and intellectual jack-of-all-trades, Gilbert Keith Chesterton. Following a U.S. visit in 1921, he wrote what is perhaps the best assessment of American ideological origins ever written. Chesterton called the United States "the only nation in the world that is founded on a creed." This ideology "is set forth with dogmatic and even theological lucidity in the Declaration of Independence; perhaps the only piece of practical politics that is also theoretical politics and also great literature. It enunciates that all men are equal in their claim to justice, that governments exist to give them that justice, and that their authority is for that reason just."[2] At its core is an extraordinary elevation of the individual citizen—his/her rights on the one hand and duties on the other.

The American ideology is commonly described in terms of a far-reaching individualism, and while that's valid, unless carefully qualified it's also misleading. The drift and consequences of American individualism are collectivist, though certainly not of a state-centered variety. It's a collectivism of citizenship. The value of each individual's shareholding depends upon the beliefs and behavior of millions of others. A sense of ownership encourages us to make sweeping claims of our rights, and to accept responsibility for the nation's health—and yet in both areas to feel vulnerable. We Americans have been less inclined than our counterparts in other democracies to turn to government for answers—in part because we've sensed that only the quality of our shared citizenship, expressed through a vast array of self-formed and self-managed groups, can sustain the type of societal life to which we aspire.

Chesterton returned to this theme, with characteristic insight, when he contrasted the U.S. experience to England's. "The idealism of England, or if you will the romance of England, has not been primarily the romance of the citizen. But the idealism of America . . . still revolves entirely around the citizen and his romance." Americans individually and collectively often fall short, Chesterton observed, in meeting their ideal of citizen rights and responsibilities. But "citizenship is still the American ideal; there is an army of actualities opposed to that ideal; but there is no ideal opposed to that ideal."[3]

Auberon Waugh has written that Chesterton saw a "natural state" or condition for Europe, and believed that "anything that threatened that state—the Industrial Revolution, banking, Marxist socialism, even social welfarism or state paternalism—was to be resisted. . . ."[4] Chesterton certainly saw much in America that he disliked, especially the power of its business system. Still, he thought it his job to understand rather than simply criticize, and he urged his readers to make the effort themselves:

> In this vision of molding many peoples into the visible image of the citizen, he [the English observer] may see a spiritual adventure that he can admire from the outside. ... He may at least understand what Jefferson and Lincoln meant, and he may possibly find some assistance in this task by reading what they said. He may realize that equality is not some crude fairy tale about all men being equally tall or equally tricky; which we not only cannot believe but cannot believe in anybody believing. It is an absolute of morals by which all men have a value invariable and indestructible and a dignity as intangible as death.[5]

This expansive sense of citizenship is enormously demanding—and not the less so for being always underrealized. The American creedal nation is permanently anxious about its custody of the ideal.

NEW ERAS, NEW CHALLENGES

Shortcomings in citizens' performance are a recurring lament—and sometimes, it must be said, for good reason. Consider, for example, John Quincy Adams's deep forebodings in his "Jubilee Address" to the New York Historical Society in 1839 upon the fiftieth anniversary of George Washington's taking office as the country's first president. The promise had been so bright, Adams observed, when the new democratic government took form under the Constitution. But, instead of withering, slavery had grown stronger and more assertive over the ensuing half century. Even beyond the deep injustices inflicted on the black population, widespread acceptance of slavery was eroding the very idea of citizenship essential in a nation that had proclaimed as self-evident that "all men are created equal . . . endowed by their Creator with certain unalienable rights, . . . among these . . . Life, Liberty, and the pursuit of Happiness."

In the late 1850s, Abraham Lincoln made this argument the core of his approach to the slavery crisis. Slavery was morally wrong, he insisted, but even more it was destructive of American nationality. Our democracy requires, Lincoln understood, great moral energy to raise citizens to higher levels of understanding of what must be done for their nation to realize its promise. Toward this, the Declaration of Independence had made a vital contribution. Lincoln called it a "standard maxim for free society, which should be familiar to all, and revered by all; constantly looked to, constantly labored for, and even though never perfectly attained, constantly approximated, and thereby constantly spreading and deepening its influence, and augmenting the happiness and value of life to all people of all colors everywhere."[6] Tragically, however, since the early years of the nineteenth century, efforts to elevate Americans' sense of what their national responsibility meant and required had flagged badly.

The deep concern over the deterioration of American citizenship that was prompted by the widespread popular acquiescence to slavery has taken many other forms since the Civil War. For example, the temperance movement of the late nineteenth and early twentieth centuries had as its immediate objective the prohibition of alcoholic beverages; but behind this lay deeper worries about an erosion of citizens' responsibility. Families were seen being anguished and community life degraded by drunkenness, and the latter was but one symptom of moral decline. In the same era, the Progressive Movement saw a crisis besetting citizenship, but understood it very differently and proposed different cures. Powerful economic interests and party "machines" had diminished government of, by, and for the people. The Progressives proposed direct primaries for picking candidates, initiatives and referenda in the legislative process, and other political reforms to refurbish the country's democracy.

Present-day worries about the depletion of vital social capital are the latest expression of this persistent American anxiety: that too many citizens—on whom the quality of our individualist democracy depends—may not be up to the job. Recessions and depressions have caused social pain and prompted national doubts, but it's the sense of broad moral decline or insufficiency that has really shaken us in every era. The triggering events this time around are well-known and deeply disturbing: a surge in rates of violent crime and drug abuse; of illegitimacy, divorce, and single-parent households—and implicated in all these a corruption of their childhood for all too many kids. Some related developments, such as the widespread use of abortion to end unwanted pregnancies, are intensely controversial; many others, though, are uniformly regretted. All saw sharp increases in their incidence in the latter half of the 1960s and early 1970s; and while there has been some recent improvement, none have returned to their pre-1960 levels.

A great many analysts locate the roots of these developments in the strong new currents that roiled our historic individualism in the quarter-century or so after World War II, leaving aspects of it altered. But here agreement breaks down. Some critics see contemporary individualism almost as the villain—as seriously, if not fatally, flawed. Robert Bellah and his colleagues argue, for example, that the self-imposed restraints that once tamed individualism in its biblical and republican forms have been weakened in today's "expressive" mutation, leaving a radically narrow and often destructive sense of individual autonomy.[7] Mary Ann Glendon, writing from a public law perspective, believes that a narrow, unnecessarily exclusionist emphasis on individual rights has diminished the society's capacity to attend satisfactorily to *responsibilities*, as opposed to *entitlements*. She sees America as being "set apart from rights discourse in other liberal democracies by its starkness and simplicity, its prodigality in bestowing the rights label, its legalistic character, its exaggerated absoluteness, its hyperindividualism, its insularity, and its silence with respect to personal, civic, and collective responsibilities."[8]

In their most extreme form, frustrations with contemporary currents have led some observers to condemn liberal individualism itself. For Robert Bork, the United States is "slouching towards Gomorrah," propelled downward by fatal flaws in its own ideas. Bork's position is a late-twentieth-century replica of that of some abolitionists in the 1850s, who despaired of democracy because of the great evil—slavery—it was sustaining.[9]

Liberal individualism continues, however, to have strong defenders. Jeffrey Hayes and S. M. Lipset take issue with communitarians who argue "that norms of responsibility to the collective whole should somehow be 'emphasized' in order to 'counter-balance' the destructive tide of individualism and selfishness in modern America. But the scale is not out of whack. Social developments in America have always been wrought with complicated contradictions, successes and failures. The way to ensure that we avoid moral decay is not to alter the culture, but rather to illuminate the ways in which we can use the moral tools with which our individualistic culture provides us so that we can fix the social problems generated by the underside of individualism."[10] I strongly agree.

If the public now showed signs of abandoning its historic inclination to join with others to meet common needs; if positive energy applied to social improvement were dissipating—leaving narrowly self-serving impulses, always present, ever more ascendant—we would in fact be facing a crisis of American citizenship. That's why it's so important for us to get the facts on social capital. The levels of engagement of individual citizens in associational activities documented here—involving millions of kids in the physical training, competition, and friendships of soccer leagues; enhancing and enjoying our natural environment; supporting school programs in almost every city and town; helping the elderly and the infirm; sustaining vigorous community religious life; etc.—clearly refute claims that individualism's "dark side" is becoming predominant.

There *is* a dark side. Tocqueville saw it more than a century and a half ago. Hayes and Lipset are right that the big contemporary challenge isn't between individualism and communitarianism, but rather between competing impulses that have always inhered in America's individualist philosophy. There isn't any viable alternative in the United States to a far-reaching individualism. The answer to its deficiencies can only be a more elevated sense of what individuals can accomplish when they accept the responsibilities of citizenship and work together more constructively.

There's no magic formula for achieving this, but surely we have lots of resources. The "nation of joiners, volunteers, and givers" idea isn't myth; the foundation built from past experience is pretty strong. What's more, present trends are encouraging. Contemporary socioeconomic developments are adding to the supply of civic resources. In today's postindustrial, knowledge-based economy, far more Americans than ever before are getting educations that help confer the skills needed for active participation. The old neighborhoods of tight physical propinquity are far less important than they used to be, but better systems of information exchange and transportation have created a great variety of new and more inclusive communities of social interaction. Greater affluence and freedom from harsh physical labor probably haven't made our lives any less stressful, but they do give more of us a chance to choose among forms of community engagement.

"Social capital" surely isn't the answer to all or most of present-day social needs. It doesn't point to an alternative to government, or tell us where private initiatives can replace those of the state. The opportunities before us if we expand our civic-mindedness are at once more modest than the claims sometimes made for it, and grander.

What, for example, if we could get 10 million people—just 5 percent of those eighteen and older—to give five hours (or an additional five hours) of their time each week for constructive volunteer activities? That would amount to an additional 50 million hours a week, and more than 2.5 billion hours in a year. No other feasible plan or program could accomplish so large an increase in community-enhancing activity. And as we've seen, current trends, far from adverse to such an achievement, are inching toward it.

Contemporary America hasn't dissipated the country's historic reserve of social capital. We really do have a chance to pass on to succeeding generations a richer supply than any predecessor enjoyed. And for all the hand-wringing, lots of Americans understand this. The record examined here hasn't been compiled by a public that's given up on the demands of citizenship.

"ON THE ROLE AND IMPORTANCE OF ASSOCIATIONS IN AMERICA"

by Alexis de Tocqueville

AUTHOR'S NOTE: All the passages that follow are Tocqueville's, from *Democracy in America*. I have simply rearranged these excerpts to tell his story more directly, and have supplied the headings.

IN NO COUNTRY in the world has the principle of association been more successfully used or applied to a greater multitude of objects than in America. Besides the permanent associations which are established by law under the names of townships, cities, and counties, a vast number of others are formed and maintained by the agency of private individuals.

A NATION OF JOINERS

The citizen of the United States is taught from infancy to rely upon his own exertions in order to resist the evils and the difficulties of life; he looks upon the social authority with an eye of mistrust and anxiety, and he claims its assistance only when he is unable to do without it. This habit may be traced even in the schools, where the children in their games are wont to submit to rules which they have themselves established, and to punish misdemeanors which they have themselves defined. The same spirit pervades every act of social life. If a stoppage occurs in a thoroughfare and the circulation of vehicles is hindered, the neighbors immediately form themselves into a deliberative body; and this extemporaneous assembly gives rise to an executive power which remedies the inconvenience before anybody has thought of recurring to a preexisting authority superior to that of the persons immediately concerned. If some public pleasure is concerned, an association is formed to give more splendor and regularity to the entertainment. Societies are formed to resist evils that are exclusively of a moral nature, as to diminish the vice of intemperance. In the United States associations are established to promote the public safety, commerce, industry, morality, and religion. There is no end which the human will despairs of attaining through the combined power of individuals united into a society. . . .[1]

The political associations that exist in the United States are only a single feature in the midst of the immense assemblage of associations in that country. Americans of all ages, all conditions, and all dispositions constantly form associations. They have not only commercial and manufacturing companies, in which all take part, but associations of a thousand other kinds, religious, moral, serious, futile, general or restricted, enormous or diminutive. The Americans make associations to give entertainments, to found seminaries, to build inns, to construct churches, to diffuse books, to send missionaries to the antipodes; in this manner they found hospitals, prisons, and schools. If it is proposed to inculcate some truth or to foster some feeling by the encouragement of a great example, they form a society. Wherever at the head of some new undertaking you see the government in France, or a man of rank in England, in the United States you will be sure to find an association.

I met with several kinds of associations in America of which I confess I had no previous notion; and I have often admired the extreme skill with which the inhabitants of the United States succeed in proposing a common object for the exertions of a great many men and in inducing them voluntarily to pursue it.

I have since traveled over England, from which the Americans have taken some of their laws and many of their customs; and it seemed to me that the principle of association was by no means so constantly or adroitly used in that country. The English often perform great things singly, whereas the Americans form associations for the smallest undertakings. It is evident that the former people consider association as a powerful means of action, but the latter seem to regard it as the only means they have of acting.

Thus the most democratic country on the face of the earth is that in which men have, in our time, carried to the highest perfection the art of pursuing in common the object of their common desire and have applied this new science to the greatest number of purposes. Is this the result of accident, or is there in reality any necessary connection between the principle of association and that of equality? . . .[2]

ON RELIGIOUS INSTITUTIONS
AND DEMOCRACY

Nothing, in my opinion, is more deserving of our attention than the intellectual and moral associations of America. The political and industrial associations of that country strike us forcibly; but the others elude our observation, or if we discover them, we understand them imperfectly because we have hardly ever seen anything of the kind. It must be acknowledged, however, that they are as necessary to the American people as the former, and perhaps more so. In democratic countries the science of association is the mother of science; the progress of all the rest depends upon the progress it has made.

Among the laws that rule human societies there is one which seems to be more precise and clear than all others. If men are to remain civilized or to become so, the art of associating together must grow and improve in the same ratio in which the equality of conditions is increased.[3]

It may fairly be believed that a certain number of Americans pursue a peculiar form of worship from habit more than from conviction. In the United States the sovereign authority is religious, and consequently hypocrisy must be common; but there is no country in the world where the Christian religion retains a greater influence over the souls of men than in America; and there can be no greater proof of its utility and of its conformity to human nature than that its influence is powerfully felt over the most enlightened and free nation of the earth.

I have remarked that the American clergy in general, without even excepting those who do not admit religious liberty, are all in favor of civil freedom; but they do not support any particular political system. They keep aloof from parties and from public affairs. In the United States religion exercises but little influence upon the laws and upon the details of public opinion; but it directs the customs of the community, and, by regulating domestic life, it regulates the state. . . .[4]

Religion in America takes no direct part in the government of society, but it must be regarded as the first of their political institutions; for if it does not impart a taste for freedom, it facilitates the use of it. Indeed, it is in this same point of view that the inhabitants of the United States themselves look upon religious belief. I do not know whether all Americans have a sincere faith in their religion—for who can search the human heart?—but I am certain that they hold it to be indispensable to the maintenance of republican institutions. This opinion is not peculiar to a class of citizens or to a party, but it belongs to the whole nation and to every rank of society. . . .[5]

There are persons in France who look upon republican institutions only as a means of obtaining grandeur; they measure the immense space that separates their vices and misery from power and riches, and they aim to fill up this gulf with ruins, that they may pass over it. These men are the *condottieri* of liberty, and fight for their own advantage, whatever the colors they wear. The republic will stand long enough, they think, to draw them up out of their present degradation. It is not to these that I address myself. But there are others who look forward to a republican form of government as a tranquil and lasting state, towards which modern society is daily impelled by the ideas and manners of the time, and who sincerely desire to prepare men to be free. When these men attack religious opinions, they obey the dictates of their passions and not of their interests. Despotism may govern without faith, but liberty cannot. Religion is much more necessary in the republic which they set forth in glowing colors than in the monarchy which they attack; it is more needed in democratic republics than in any others. How is it possible that society should escape destruction if the moral tie is not strengthened in proportion as the political tie is relaxed? And what can be done with a people who are their own masters if they are not submissive to the Deity?[6]

ON THE INTERACTION OF THE CIVIL AND THE POLITICAL

There is only one country on the face of the earth where the citizens enjoy unlimited freedom of association for political purposes. This same country is the only one in the world where the continual exercise of the right of association has been introduced into civil life and where all the advantages which civilization can confer are procured by means of it.

In all the countries where political associations are prohibited, civil associations are rare. It is hardly probable that this is the result of accident, but the inference should rather be that there is a natural and perhaps a necessary connection between these two kinds of associations.

Certain men happen to have a common interest in some concern; either a commercial undertaking is to be managed, or some speculation in manufactures to be tried: they meet, they combine, and thus, by degrees, they become familiar with the principle of association. The greater the multiplicity of small affairs, the more do men, even without knowing it, acquire facility in prosecuting great undertakings in common.

Civil associations, therefore, facilitate political association; but on the other hand, political association singularly strengthens and improves associations for civil purposes. In civil life every man may, strictly speaking, fancy that he can provide for his own wants; in politics he can fancy no such thing. When a people, then, have any knowledge of public life, the notion of association and the wish to coalesce present themselves every day to the minds of the whole community; whatever natural repugnance may restrain men from acting in concert, they will always be ready to combine for the sake of a party. Thus political life makes the love and practice of association more general; it imparts a desire of union and teaches the means of combination to numbers of men who otherwise would have always lived apart. . . .[7]

Is it enough to observe these things separately, or should we not discover the hidden tie that connects them? In their political associations the Americans, of all conditions, minds, and ages, daily acquire a general taste for association and grow accustomed to the use of it. There they meet together in large numbers, they converse, they listen to one another, and they are mutually stimulated to all sorts of undertakings. They afterwards transfer to civil life the notions they have thus acquired and make them subservient to a thousand purposes. Thus it is by the enjoyment of a dangerous freedom that the Americans learn the art of rendering the dangers of freedom less formidable. . . .[8]

THE GOVERNMENTAL CHALLENGE

There are no countries in which associations are more needed to prevent the despotism of faction or the arbitrary power of a prince than those which are democratically constituted. In aristocratic nations the body of the nobles and the wealthy are in themselves natural associations which check the abuses of power. In countries where such associations do not exist, if private individuals cannot create an artificial and temporary substitute for them I can see no permanent protection against the most galling tyranny; and a great people may be oppressed with impunity by a small faction or by a single individual. . . .'

A government might perform the part of some of the largest American companies, and several states, members of the Union, have already attempted it; but what political power could ever carry on the vast multitude of lesser undertakings which the American citizens perform every day, with the assistance of the principle of association? It is easy to foresee that the time is drawing near when man will be less and less able to produce, by himself alone, the commonest necessaries of life. The task of the governing power will therefore perpetually increase, and its very efforts will extend it every day. The more it stands in the place of associations, the more will individuals, losing the notion of combining together, require its assistance: these are causes and effects that unceasingly create each other. Will the administration of the country ultimately assume the management of all the manufactures which no single citizen is able to carry on? And if a time at length arrives when, in consequence of the extreme subdivision of landed property, the soil is split into an infinite number of parcels, so that it can be cultivated only by companies of tillers, will it be necessary that the head of the government should leave the helm of state to follow the plow? The morals and the intelligence of a democratic people would be as much endangered as its business and manufactures if the government ever wholly usurped the place of private companies. . . .'[10]

AN HONOR ROLL OF AMERICAN PHILANTHROPY

T HE LADD REPORT has documented the extensive charitable giving of Americans in all income groups. These data are, unavoidably, only aggregates. They can't identify individual efforts—the variety of philanthropy by millions of ordinary citizens to our churches, community food banks, United Way campaigns, and youth organizations. We can sum up the totals, but we can't list the individuals.

The honor roll of charitable giving in the pages that follow is limited, then, to big contributions by individual givers, corporations, and foundations, and to the charities that are the largest recipients of private support. These are all worthy parts of the honor roll of charitable giving, but they leave out the most important unit in American philanthropy—the ordinary citizen of average means.

Contributions by Individuals of $1 Million or More,
January 1996 to June 1998
(Source: *Slate Magazine*, "Slate 60")

Giver	Amount (in millions of dollars)	Recipient
Turner, Ted	1,000	United Nations, and Environmental and Population-Related Organizations

Giver	Amount	Recipient
	(in millions of dollars)	
Soros, George	531	The city of Baltimore, Needle-Exchange Programs, Robin Hood Foundation, and Russia (public health projects)
Stowers, James E. Jr. & Virginia	327	Stowers Institute for Medical Research
Gates, Bill & Melinda	243	Gates Library Foundation, Johns Hopkins University, Friends of Mandela Childrens Fund, Catholic Archdiocese of Seattle, Cambridge University, Lakeside School (Seattle), Access to Voluntary and Safe Contraception, Pacific Science Center (Seattle), Multiservice Centers, Operation Smile
Mann, Alfred E.	200	University of Southern California, and University of California at Los Angeles
Skaggs, Samuel & Aline	100	Scripps Research Institute
Soros, George	100	Emma Lazarus Fund, Misc.
Abramson, Leonard & Madlyn	100	University of Pennsylvania
Weill, Sanford I. & Joan	100	Cornell University
Wolfson, Mitchell Jr.	76	Florida International University
Williams, Arthur L. & Angela	70	Liberty University
Wattis, Phyllis	67	Fine Arts Museums of San Francisco, San Francisco Museum of Modern Art, California Academy of Sciences, San Francisco Art Institute, Exploratorium (San Francisco), Utah Museum of Art, Berkeley Museum of Art, San Francisco Symphony, and San Francisco Opera Association
Perls, Klaus G. & Amelia	60	Metropolitan Museum of Art
Galvin, Robert W.	60	Illinois Institute of Technology
Pritzker Families	60	Illinois Institute of Technology
Opperman, Dwight	54	Drake Universtiy
Forstmann, Theodore J.	50	Children's Scholarship Fund
Walton, John T.	50	Children's Scholarship Fund
Forstmann, Theodore, J.	50	Children's Scholarship Fund
Lewis, Peter B.	49	Solomon R. Guggenheim Foundation, and Case Western Reserve University
Goldschmied, Gonda	45	UCLA
Gonda, Leslie & Susan	45	Mayo Clinic
Fisher, Richard, Susan Soros, & Leon Levy	42	Bard College
Arison Family	40	New World Symphony

(continued)

Giver	Amount (in millions of dollars)	Recipient
Huntsman, Jon M.	40	University of Pennsylvania
Druckenmiller, Stanley	36	Bowdoin College
Frey, Eugene & Mary	34	St. Paul Foundation, and Catholic Community Foundation
Loker, Katherine B.	34	University of Southern California, and Harvard University
Hobby Family	33	Music Hall Foundation, and Rice University
Mailman Family	33	Columbia University
Allen, Paul G.	32	Starbright Pediatric Foundation, University of Washington, Stanford University, Survivors of the Shoah Foundation, Lakeside School, Burke Museum, Children's museum, Corporate Council for the Arts, Habitat for Humanity, Lopez Community Center, Pacific Northwest Ballet, Seattle Art Museum, Overlake Hospital Foundation, Seniors Making Art, Four Winds Westward Ho Camp, Seattle Public Library Foundation, Doernbecher Children's Hospital, and Whitman College
Dedman, Robert H. Sr. & Nancy	32	Southern Methodist University
McVaney, C. Edward & Carole	32	University of Nebraska
Gates, Bill & Melinda	31	University of Washington, Planned Parenthood Federation of America Inc., Program for Appropriate Technology in Health, AVSC International, St. George's School, U.N. Population Fund, Population Council, CARE, International Aids Vaccine Initiative, Eastern Virginia Medical School, Columbia University, City Year Seattle/King County, and Bellevue Art Museum
Bass, Robert M. and Anne	30	Yale University, Duke University
Lang, Eugene M.	30	Swarthmore College
Schreyer, William A. & Joan	30	Pennsylvania State University
Soros, George	30	Pushkin Project, National Association for Public Interest Law, and Tides Foundation
Zicklin, Lawrence & Carol	28	City University of New York
Gates, Bill	27	Harvard University, University of Washington

(continued)

Giver	Amount (in millions of dollars)	Recipient
McDonnell, John F. & James S.	27	Washington University (School of Medicine), St. Louis Children's Hospital, and Washington University (for three professorships)
Buntrock, Dean, Rosemarie, & Family	26	St. Olaf College
Knight, Philip H.	25	University of Oregon
Lerner, Alfred	25	Columbia University
Bright, H. R. "Bum"	25	Texas A & M
Lewin, Bernard & Edith	25	Los Angeles County Museum of Art
Ovitz, Michael & Judy	25	UCLA Medical Center
Smith, Carl W. & Hunter	25	University of Virginia
Stata, Ray & Maria	25	Massachusetts Institute of Technology
Fisher, Donald & Doris	25	Edison Project
Kroc, Joan B.	25	University of San Diego
Moore, Darla	25	University of South Carolina
Pew, Mary & Robert	25	Community Foundation for Palm Beach and Martin Counties
Ritchie, Daniel L.	25	University of Denver
Soros, Paul & Daisy	24	A trust to help underwrite American graduate education for immigrants and their children
Kelley, E. W.	23	Indiana University
Lee, Thomas H.	22	Harvard University
Weatherhead, Albert J. & Celia S.	21	Harvard University
Leeds, Gerard & Lilo	21	Institute for Student Achievement
Knafel, Sidney	20	Harvard University
Nicholas, Peter M.	20	Duke University
Heinz, The Family of the late Sen. H. John	20	To establish the Heinz Research Center
Rose, Frederick P. & Sandra	20	American Museum of Natural History
Pigott Family, Braun Family, & Lane Family	20	Stanford University
Behring, Kenneth	20	Smithsonian Institution
Bren, Donald	20	University of California at Santa Barbara & University of California at Irvine
Cullman, Lewis & Dorothy	20	Yale University & New York Public Library
Duffield, David A.	20	Cornell University
Ford, Gerald J.	20	Southern Methodist University
Ford, Josephine	20	Center for Creative Studies
Kauffman, John P. & Ann	20	College of William and Mary
Allen, Herbert A.	20	Williams College
Davis Family, The J. E.	20	Jacksonville University

(continued)

Giver	Amount (in millions of dollars)	Recipient
Dreyfoos, Alexander W. Jr.	20	Massachusetts Institute of Technology and Raymond F. Kravis Center for the Performing Arts
Fuqua, J. B.	20	Duke University
McNair, Robert C. & Janice	20	University of South Carolina
Rogers, James E.	20	University of Arizona
Casey, Betty Brown	18	Washington Opera
Price, Michael F.	18	University of Oklahoma
Rapoport, Bernard	18	University of Texas at Austin
Mitte, Roy F., & Joann Cole	18	Southwest Texas State University
Leepa, Allen & Isabelle	17	St. Petersburg Junior College
Rose, Sandra Priest & Frederick	17	New York Public Library
Huntsman, Jon M., Karen, & Family	17	The University of Pennsylvania, Brigham Young University, University of Utah, Southern Utah University
Jamail, Joseph D. and Lee	16	The University of Texas at Austin, Museum of Fine Arts (Houston), Baylor College of Medicine, Rice University, University of Texas M.D. Anderson Cancer Center, University of Texas Health Science Center, and the Lee and Joseph Jamail Foundation
Lerner, Alfred & Norma	16	Cleveland Clinic Foundation
Lee, Chong-Moon	15	San Francisco Public Library
Gleacher, Eric	15	University of Chicago School of Business
Feinberg, Reuben	15	Northwestern Memorial Hospital
Kimmel, Sidney & Rena Rowan	15	United States Holocaust Museum and the Thomas Jefferson University
Ourso, J.	15	Louisiana State University College of Business Administration
Lewis, Peter B.	15	Case Western Reserve University
Graziadio, George L. and Reva	15	Pepperdine University
Karmanos, Peter	15	Barbara Ann Karmanos Cancer Institute
Moore, Gordon E. and Betty	15	University of California, Berkeley
Scandling, William F.	15	Hobart and William Smith College and University of Rochester
Kroc, Joan	15	Flood victims in Red River, ND
Marcus, Bernard	15	Atlanta Jewish Federation
Jacobs, Irwin M. & Joan K.	15	University of California at San Diego
Osher, Bernard	15	University of California at San Francisco, Bates College, Bowdoin College, Colby College, and the University of Maine
Silverman, Henry R.	15	University of Pennsylvania

(continued)

Giver	Amount	Recipient
	(in millions of dollars)	
Smith, Robert H.	15	University of Maryland at College Park
Gatton, M. (Bill)	14	University of Kentucky
Manderson, Lewis M. Jr.	14	University of Alabama, College of Commerce and Business Administration
Weiss, George	14	Medical College of Georgia
Berrie, Russell	14	Columbia University
Allen, Paul	14	Nature Conservancy, Trust for Public Land, Seattle Public Library, Cable Museum, and Friends of Opal Creek
Baker, Lenox Jr. and Frances Watt	13	Johns Hopkins University School of Medicine and Davidson College
Hilbert, Stephen & Tomisue	13	Indiana Symphony Orchestra & Indianapolis Zoo
Feinberg, Abraham	13	Brandeis University
Brown, Rubin	12	UCLA Children's Hospital
Warren, William C.	12	Columbia University
Pratt, Edmund & Jeanette	12	Long Island University
Goergen, Robert B. and Pamela	11	University of Rochester
Sykes, John & Susan	11	University of Tampa, United Way of Hillsborough County, & Tampa Police Station
Davis, Kathryn Wasserman	11	Wellesley College
Tarble, Pat	11	Carthage College
Burden Family, The Carter & Susan	11	Pierpont Morgan Library
Ballmer, Steve	10	Harvard University
Batten, Frank	10	University of Virginia
Druckenmiller, Fiona Biggs and Stanley	10	Spence School
Boler, John and Mary Jo	10	John Carroll University
Borgenicht, Jack	10	College of William and Mary
Davis, Kathryn W.	10	Harvard University
Eck, Frank	10	Notre Dame University
Greenebaum, Stewart and Marlene	10	University of Maryland Medical Center
Irving, Herbert	10	Columbia-Presbyterian Medical Center
Lauder, Leonard	10	University of Pennsylvania
Laurie, William	10	University of Missouri
Musser, Warren V. (Pete)	10	Lehigh University
Pope, Lois	10	Miami Project to Cure Paralysis
Vagelos, Roy and Diana	10	University of Pennsylvania
Slane, Henry P.	10	Bradley University
Walsh, Willam D.	10	Fordham University
Alsdorf, Marilynn	10	Art Institute of Chicago

(continued)

Giver	Amount (in millions of dollars)	Recipient
Daniels, Bill	10	City of Denver
Dayton, Bruce & Ruth	10	Minneapolis Institute of Arts
Eller, Karl	10	University of Arizona
Gagnon, Neil & Lois, and Charles E. & Cornelia Hugel	10	Lafayette College
Georgen, Robert B.	10	Wharton School
Goldman, Richard & Rhoda	10	University of California at Berkeley
Graham, William B. & Catherine V.	10	University of Chicago
Hauser, Rita A. & Gustav M.	10	Harvard University
Keller, Dennis J.	10	Princeton University
McAfee, James T. Jr. & Carolyn Townsend	10	Mercer University
McCaw Family	10	Lakeside School
Michener, James	10	University of Texas
Nessel, Barbara & Melvin	10	Massachusetts General Hospital Cancer Center
Nippert, Louise Dieterle	10	Cincinnati Symphony Orchestra
Quadracci, Harry V. & Betty	10	Milwaukee Art Museum
Stine, Harry H.	10	McPherson College (Kans.)
Tutor, Ronald	10	University of Southern California
Underwood, David M.	10	Phillips Academy
Vagelos, P. Roy & Diana	10	University of Pennsylvania
Zuckerman, Mel & Enid	10	University of Arizona
Zell, Sam	10	Wharton School
Annenberg, Walter & Leonore	10	Independence Mall
Caspersen, Finn M. W.	10	Peddie School
Clark, A. James	10	Johns Hopkins University
Ford, Josephine	10	Henry Ford Health System
Haas Family, The	10	National Park Service
Jamail, Joe & Lee	10	Texas Heart Institute
Milstein, Philip L.	10	Columbia University
Nelson, James K. B. & Audrey	10	Texas A & M University at College Station
Tang, Oscar L.	10	Phillips Academy
Wang, Charles	10	Operation Smile
Wasserman, Lew & Edith	10	UCLA
Weissman, George & Mildred	10	City University of New York
Stabile, Vincent A.	9	Pratt Institute
Wallace, David W. & Jean McLean	9	Yale University
Clay, Landon T.	9	Harvard University
Greenlee, Robert & Diane	9	Iowa State University

(continued)

Giver	Amount	Recipient
	(in millions of dollars)	
Morsani, Frank and Carol	8	Community Foundation of Greater Tampa
Saunders, Donald L.	8	Combined Jewish Philanthropies
Galbraith, John & Rosemary	8	Florida International Museum
Boyer, Eleanor	8	Church of The Immaculate Conception, and the Town of Somerville, N.J.
Kripke, Myer & Dorothy	8	Jewish Theological Seminary, and Reconstructionist Rabbinical College
Martin, Lee & Geraldine	8	Massachusetts Institute of Technology
Prothro, Charles & Elizabeth Perkins	8	Southern Methodist University, and Wofford College
Shehan, Jean D.	8	National Audubon Society
Belfer, Robert A. & Renee	8	Harvard University
Burkle, Ron	8	Walt Disney Concert Hall
Perkinson, C. D. & Pat	8	Millikin University
Howe, Stanley and Helen	7	Iowa State University
Carreker, James R.	7	Georgia Institute of Technology
Drobny, Sheldon & Anita	7	University of Illinois
Blanton, Laura Lee & Jack	7	Southern Methodist University
Broad, Eli	7	Walt Disney Concert Hall, and Michigan State University
Hines, Gerald D. & Family	7	University of Houston
Horvitz, Leonard & Joan	7	Rainbow Babies & Children's Hospital
James, Ardis & Robert	7	University of Nebraska at Lincoln, and International Quilt Study Center
Fulton, Stanley	7	University of Nevada at Las Vegas
Little, Carol & Leonard Rabinowitz	7	Accelerated School
Howe, Wesley J.	7	Stevens Institute of Technology
Lindner, Carl	7	University of Cincinnati, and Catholic Urban Schools
Price, Sol	7	San Diego Foundation
Wattis, Phyllis	7	San Francisco Art Institute, San Francisco Museum of Modern Art
Langone, Kenneth G.	7	New York University
Michener, James	6	Three cultural institutions in Doylestown, Penn.
Culverhouse, Joy	6	University of South Florida
Newcomb, Bernard	6	Oregon State University
Eastwood, Clint & Maggie	6	Big Sur Land Trust
Fisher, Max, Family	6	Detroit Symphony Orchestra
Frankel, Samuel & Jean	6	Detroit Symphony Orchestra
Isenberg, Eugene & Ronnie	6	University of Massachusetts at Amherst
Kleist, Peter & Eleanore	6	Ohio Wesleyan University, and Claflin College
Markin, David R.	6	Bradley University
Moores, John & Rebecca	6	San Diego State University

(continued)

Giver	Amount	Recipient
	(in millions of dollars)	
Morgridge, John & Tashia	6	Alverno College
Schulz, Charles & Jean	6	Sonoma State University, and National D-Day Memorial
Weis, Janet, & The Rooke Family	6	Bucknell University
Gleacher, Eric J.	6	Northwestern University
Behrakis, George	6	Northeastern University
Murray, Ray & Nancy	6	Community Foundation of Tampa Bay
Wohlers, Albert & Jane	6	University of Illinois
Shapiro, Carl & Ruth	6	Museum of Fine Arts
Barksdale, James L.	5	University of Mississippi
Blank, Arthur	5	Babson College
Bond, William Jr.	5	University of Notre Dame
Erb, Frederick and Barbara	5	University of Michigan Business School
Capozzolo, Anthony	5	University of Southern California
Dannheisser, Elaine	5	Museum of Modern Art
Fitzgerald, William T.	5	University of Akron
Gault, Stanley C.	5	College of Wooster
Geffen, David	5	Museum of Contemporary Art
Halle, Claus M. and Marianne	5	Emory University
Jordan, Gerald R.	5	Harvard College
Marx, Louis Jr.	5	Middlebury College
Schulz, Charles & Jean	5	Sonoma State University
Sturm, Donald and Susan	5	University of Denver
Montgomery, Gratia (Topsy) R.	5	Woods Hole Oceanographic Institute
Palevsky, Max and Ellen	5	University of Chicago
Ward, Tom and Sch'ree	5	Anderson University
Wise, David and Karen	5	Allegheny College
Vernon, Lillian M.	5	New York University
Lind, Elizabeth B.	5	Northwestern University
Gotsen, Lloyd E.	5	Princeton University
Pappajohn, John and Mary	5	University of Iowa, Drake University, Iowa State University, North Iowa Area Community College, and University of Northern Iowa
Kluge, John W.	5	University of Virginia
Abele, John	5	Educational programs
Baskin, Jack	5	University of California at Santa Cruz
Blank, Arthur	5	Atlanta Jewish Federation
Corbett, Patricia	5	Cincinnati Symphony Orchestra
Cornell, George & Harriet	5	Palm Beach Zoo
Disney, Roy E. & Patty	5	Walt Disney Concert Hall

(continued)

Giver	Amount	Recipient
	(in millions of dollars)	
Doyle, Frank M., Family	5	Huntington Beach Union High School District
Elkowitz, Edward	5	New York Institute of Technology
Feinstein, Alan Shawn	5	Tufts University, Roger Williams University, and Johnson & Wales University
Gill, Linda & Jack	5	University of Kentucky
Green, Don & Maureen	5	Sonoma State University
Hintz, Edward R. & Helen	5	Pennsylvania State University
Hunt, Lamar & Norma	5	Southern Methodist University
Hunt, Ray & Nancy	5	Southern Methodist University
Iacocca, Lee	5	Lehigh University
Nanovic, Robert S. & Elizabeth	5	University of Notre Dame
Neuberger, Roy R.	5	State University of New York College at Purchase
Perelman, Raymond & Ruth	5	Toward a new performing-arts center in Philadelphia
Peterson, Peter G.	5	Council on Foreign Relations
Prentiss, Jim & Carol	5	Memphis Zoo
Rennert, Ira & Ingeborg	5	Yeshiva University, and Barnard College
Riordan, Richard J.	5	Walt Disney Concert Hall
Robinson, David & Valerie	5	Carver Complex
Simpson, Barclay & Sharon	5	University of Washington
Stephens, Jack	5	Arkansas Arts Center
Waggoner, J. Virgil & June	5	University of Texas at Austin
Weiner, Michael & Zena	5	Mount Sinai Medical Center
Wilson, Bob & Marion	5	University of California at Los Angeles
Wilson, Gary & Barbera Thornhill	5	Duke University
Worrell, Anne Rowell & T. Eugene	5	Virginia Intermont College
Wrigley, William T., Family	5	University of Southern California
Sweetland, John W.	5	University of Michigan
Albertson, Kathryn	5	Albertson College
Tisch, Laurence A. & Preston Robert	5	Children's Zoo
Berkman, Lilllian R. & Jack N.	5	Harvard University
Rand, William	5	Jewish Museum
Wish, Barry & Oblio	5	Bowdoin College
Berrie, Russell & Angelica	5	Englewood Hospital and Medical Center
Blanton, Jack S. & Laura Lee	5	Jack S. Blanton Museum of Art
Bloomberg, Michael R.	5	Institute for Advanced Study
Cain, Mary & Gordon	5	Rice University
Davis, Jerry & Judith	5	University of Florida

(continued)

Giver	Amount (in millions of dollars)	Recipient
DeGeorge, Lawrence J. & Florence	5	Juvenile Diabetes Foundation International
Goldman, Richard & Rhoda	5	National Geographic Society
Gongaware, Donald & Pat	5	Indiana State University
Greif, Lloyd	5	University of Southern California
Hauser, Rita	5	Harvard University
Helppie, The Richard D. & Leslie S., Family	5	Children's Hospital of Michigan
Holtz, Fana	5	Jackson Children's Hospital
Inlow, Anita C.	5	Indiana University
Kluge, John W.	5	University of Virginia
Landau, Emily Fisher	5	Yeshiva University
Longaberger Family Foundation	5	Ohio State University
McGraw, Harold W. Jr.	5	Princeton University
Molinari, Arthur A.	5	University of the Pacific
Morgan, Ellison (Eli) C.	5	Self Enhancement Inc.
Murphy, Joseph M. & Joann	5	Iona State College
Myers, Charles C. & Romona	5	University of Dubuque
Neuberger, Roy R.	5	Purchase College
Pasquerilla, Frank, and Family	5	Pennsylvania State University
Perelman, Ronald O.	5	Solomon R. Guggenheim Foundation
Prior, Cornelius B. Jr.	5	College of the Holy Cross
Rasmuson, Elmer & Mary Louise	5	Virginia Mason Research Center
Riley, Harold	5	Southwestern Baptist Theological Seminary
Foss, William & Juliana W. Thompson	5	Harvard University
Vilar, Alberto W.	5	Washington & Jefferson College
Weeks, Katherine	5	Baylor School
Wunderman, Severin	5	Survivors of the Shoah Visual History Foundation
Renk, Walter, Martha, Richard, and Sharon	4	University of Wisconsin at Madison
Walton, Helen Robson	4	University of Arkansas
Harrell, Frankie & Stan	4	Metropolitan Ministries
Hazy, Steven and Christine	4	Dixie College
Tsuzuki, Yasuhisa & Kimiko	4	Harvard Graduate School of Education
Udvar-Hazy, Steven & Christine	4	Dixie College
Vlasic, Robert J.	4	University of Michigan

(continued)

Giver	Amount	Recipient
	(in millions of dollars)	
St. Gregory's Abbey, The Monks of	4	St. Gregory's College
Bernhard, A. Van H.	4	Quinnipiac College
Gerry, Alan	4	Massachusetts General Hospital
Hudgens, Scott & Jacqueline	4	Gwinnett Council for the Arts, Gwinnett High School, Rainbow Village, Gwinnett Children's Shelter, and Potosi Island
King, Stephen & Tabitha	4	University of Maine
Loudermilk, R. Charles Sr.	4	University of North Carolina at Chapel Hill
Peterson, Bill & Jane	4	State of Wisconsin
Robertson, Julian & Josie	4	Hollins College, and Rhodes College
Wright, Robert J. & Mary	4	Austin College
Bigelow, Robert T. & Diana	4	University of Nevada at Las Vegas
Little, Judy & Brian	4	Colgate University
Benaroya, Larry & Sherry and Family	4	Virginia Mason Research Center
Pamplin, Robert B. Sr. & Robert B. Jr.	4	Virginia Polytechnic Institute and State University
Turner, Cal Jr.	4	Vanderbilt Divinity School, and Belmont University
Alfond, Harold & Ted	3	Rollins College
McMichael, Dalton	3	Elon College
Bloomberg, Michael R.	3	Harvard University
Fletcher, Alphonse Jr.	3	Harvard University
Fraser, Helen & Richard	3	Museum of Fine Arts
Grossman, Burton & Miriam	3	Johns Hopkins University School of Medicine
Kroc, Joan B.	3	University of San Diego
Richmond, Jack & Marge Raymond	3	University of Illinois at Urbana-Champaign
Philippe, Thomas & Joan	3	Indiana Wesleyan University
Lavietes, Raymond P.	3	Harvard College
Meyerhoff, Harvey "Bud" & Lyn	3	Johns Hopkins University
Baker, Frances Watt & Lenox Jr.	3	Davidson College
Gorr, Ivan	3	University of Toledo College of Business Administration
Koch, David & Barbara	3	University of St. Thomas
Hull, Andre, & Duvahl Ridgway	3	Longwood College
Setnor, Jules & Rose	3	Syracuse University
Anderson Family	3	Chapman University
Beckmen, Arnold	3	Chapman University

(continued)

Giver	Amount	Recipient
	(in millions of dollars)	
Boone, George & Marylou	3	Huntington Library Art Collections and Botanical Gardens
Buckman, Robert & Joyce	3	Asbury Theological Seminary
DeVos, Richard	3	Lee College
Embrey, J. Lindsay Jr. & Bobbie	3	Southern Methodist University
Forstman, Ted	3	Washington Scholarship Fund
Gragnani, Charlotte	3	Providence College
Hamilton, Dorrance	3	Thomas Jefferson University
Higley, Albert M.	3	Kenyon College
Hoeft, Leonard & Mary Lou	3	University of Illinois at Champaign-Urbana
Klein, Walter C. & Virgilia H. Pancoast	3	Harvard University
Lewis, Adam J.	3	Oberlin College
Lewis, Marilyn & Drew	3	Ursinus College
McCombs, B.J. (Red) & Charline	3	University of Texas at Austin
Munroe Sisters: Julia Munroe Woodward, Mary Gray Munroe Cobey & Margaret Munroe Thrower	3	Wesleyan College
Noel, Melissa	3	University of Illinois at Champaign-Urbana
Pettus, Sherrill & Jo Ann	3	Southern Methodist University
Ragsdale, Robert	3	St. Edward's University
Robb, Dink	3	First United Methodist Church, Electra Public Library, and Electra High School
Salick, Bernard	3	Queens College
Saltzman, Arnold A.	3	Columbia University
Sebits, Carl & Dixie	3	Friends University
Tolleson, John & Debbie	3	Southern Methodist University
Walton, John	3	Washington Scholarship Fund
Stephens, Thelma	3	Idaho State University
Warner, Jack	3	Unversity of Alabama
Hobbs, Elisabeth A. & Emily H. Fisher, Nancy Aronson, & an anonymous woman	3	Harvard University
Lessin, Robert H., & Naida S. Wharton	3	Harvard University
Quinney, S.J., Family	3	University of Utah
Smith, Steve	3	Michigan State University
Strangeland, Roger	3	St. John's Northwestern Military Academy
Trulaske, Robert J. Sr.	3	University of Missouri at Columbia

(continued)

Giver	Amount (in millions of dollars)	Recipient
Waldron, William G.	3	Gulf of Maine Aquarium Development Corp.
Wasserstein Family, The Morris	2	Harvard Law School
Stoops, Emery & Joyce King	2	University of Southern California
Swift, Thomas E. III & Dottie	2	Shelton School and Evaluation Center
Nelson, Warren & Pat	2	Carroll College
Wehr, Robert & James R.	2	Southwest Missouri State University
Arnold, Edward & Suzanne	2	University of Notre Dame
Black, Scott M. & Barbara C.	2	Johns Hopkins University
Cray, Bud & Richard	2	Benedictine College
Fisher, George M. C. & Ann	2	University of Illinois at Urbana-Champaign
Glidenhorn, Joseph B. & Alma	2	University of Maryland at College Park
Harmon, Adrian & Margaret	2	Central Missouri State University
Hayworth, Pauline Lewis	2	Queens College
Rennart, Inge & Ira	2	New York University
Rose, Marilyn Gaddis & Stephen David	2	State University of New York at Binghamton
Hewlett Family, The William	2	Menlo College
Johnson, Thomas P.	2	Rollins College
Hultquist, Timothy & Cindy	2	Macalester College
Lee, Desmond Jr.	2	St. Louis Art Museum
Landau, Ralph	2	Massachusetts Institute of Technology
Sartz, Frank	2	Palmer College of Chiropractic
McGinnis, Gerald E.	2	University of Illinois at Urbana-Champaign
Miller, Jeffrey J. & Paula	2	University of Southern California
Piper, Ione	2	University of Southern California School of Public Administration
Sosland Family Foundation	2	Harvard University
Smith, Carolyn and David, Robert, Duncan and Fred	2	Johns Hopkins University
Tiefenthaler, Marjorie & Lorin	2	University of Wisconsin at Madison
McMaster, Harold, Helen & Philip Gardner	2	University of Toledo
Mario, Ernest & Mildred	2	Duke University
Greenspun Family	2	University of Nevada at Las Vegas
Reinsdorf, Jerry & William Wirtz	2	Malcolm X College (Chicago)
Mason, Major-Gen. Raymond E. & Margaret	2	Ohio State University

(continued)

Giver	Amount (in millions of dollars)	Recipient
Cornell, George & Harriet	2	Cornell Fine Arts Museum at Rollins College (Fla.)
Coleman, David D. (Mickey)	2	University of Tennessee at Memphis
Brehm, William K. & Ernst Volgenau	2	United States Naval Academy
Dedman, Robert	2	University of North Texas
Elmaleh, Victor	2	University of Virginia
Fuqua, B.	2	Atlanta Committee for The Olympic Games
Georges, John & Lou	2	University of Illinois at Urbana-Champaign
Hanson, John K. & Luise	2	Waldorf College (Iowa)
Harris, Kenneth L.	2	Faulkner University (Ala.)
Johnson, George Dean Jr. & Susan	2	Wofford College (S.C.)
Leatherby, Ralph & Eleanor	2	Chapman University
Dayton, Ruth Stricker & Bruce	2	Macalester College
Mellencamp, John	2	Indiana University
Thumel, William Jr.	2	University of Baltimore
Oleary, Richard E. & Ann	2	University of Illinois at Urbana-Champaign
O'Quinn, John	2	To help build a counseling center for sexually abused children
Reilly, William F.	2	University of Notre Dame
Sylvester, Harcourt Jr.	2	Florida Philharmonic
Toner, Howard & Kathleen	2	Saint Mary's University
Winter, Richard E.	2	Canisius College
Becher, F. James Jr., & Michael Weaver	2	University of North Carolina at Greensboro
Bennett, William	2	University of Nevada at Las Vegas
Stanley, John R. & Eileen	2	Baylor College of Medicine
Cross, Wright W. & Annie Rea	2	University of Southern Mississippi
Flores, James C., & Cherie Flores	2	Louisiana State University
Rucks, Catherine & William W. IV	2	Louisiana State Unversity
Pope, Bill J. & Margaret M.	2	Brigham Young University, and Utah Valley State College
Attallah, Fahmy & Donna	2	University of Southern California
Bagwell, Clarice	2	Kennesaw State University
Berman, Lyle & Janice, Nathan & Theresa	2	University of Minnesota
Boccardo, James F. & Lorraine	2	San Jose State University
Burke, John & Kathryn	2	Milwaukee Art Museum, and Spirit of Milwaukee

(continued)

Giver	Amount (in millions of dollars)	Recipient
Colbeth, Douglas P. & Margaret	2	University of Illinois at Champaign-Urbana
De Santis, Carl	2	Florida Atlantic University
Dingman, Michael D.	2	University of Maryland
Failing, Charlotte	2	Wayne State University
Fantle, Sally M.	2	Augustana College
Filo, David, & Chih-Yuan (Jerry) Yang	2	Stanford University
Fuqua, J. B.	2	Crystal Cathedral
Gillings, Dennis	2	University of North Carolina at Chapel Hill
Gornto, Barbara	2	Old Dominion University
Green, Steve & Dorothea	2	Florida International University
Halloran, John	2	Niagara University
Hank, Joyce McMahon	2	St. Mary's College
Herzfeld, Richard & Ethel	2	Milwaukee Art Museum
Hicks, David & Ann	2	University of North Florida
Inman, High M. & Elizabeth	2	PACE Academy
Junker, Edward P. III & Barbara	2	Pennsylvania State University at Erie—Behrend College, Pennsylvania State University at Erie
Karmanos, Peter Jr. & Debra Glendening	2	Grady Memorial Hospital
Kerr, Banks D.	2	University of North Carolina at Chapel Hill
Klieger, Elaine D.	2	Medical College of Wisconsin
Pawley, Dennis & Carlotta	2	Oakland University
Proctor, Fred L. & Myrtle R.	2	Greensboro College
Pyle, Thomas & Judith	2	University of Wisconsin at Madison
Sharf, Stephan & Rita	2	Oakland University
Shirley, Jon & Mary	2	Bellevue Art Museum
Shlafer, Shirley	2	Detroit Symphony Orchestra
Short, Harold	2	Colorado State University
Snider, Ed	2	University of Pennsylvania
Spanos, Alex G.	2	American Red Cross, and California State University at Sacramento
Stead, Jerre & Mary Joy	2	Garrett-Evangelical Theological Seminary
Winfrey, Oprah	2	A Better Chance, and Morehouse College
Wright, Crispus (Chris) Attucks	2	University of Southern California
Schwenck, Harold Jr.	2	University of Connecticut
Simpkins, Alan & Phyllis	2	San Jose State University
Handleman, David & Marion	2	Detroit Symphony Orchestra
Papitto, Ralph R.	2	Roger Williams University
Butler, Ernest & Sarah	2	Austin Museum of Art

(continued)

Giver	Amount	Recipient
	(in millions of dollars)	
Collins, Priscilla Bullitt	2	Vassar College
Cudahy, Michael J.	2	Johns Hopkins University
Drugas, Theodore	2	University of Illinois at Chicago
Foster, Ellen D.	2	University of Illinois at Peoria
Galter, Dollie	2	Lutheran General Hospital/Advocate Health Care
Gonzales, Arthur H.	2	University of Southern Colorado
Helmsley, Leona M.	2	Burned Churches Fund
Hudson, Bill Jr.	2	William Carey College
Irmas Family	2	University of Southern California
Johnson, James A.	2	Brookings Institution
Martin, James F.	2	Clemson University
McCain, Warren & Bernie	2	Albertson College
McKerley, Forrest D.	2	University of New Hampshire
Moore, Gordon E.	2	Oregon Graduate Institute of Science and Technology
Neag, Raymond & Lynn	2	University of Connecticut
Petersilie, Frank & Beth	2	Appalachian State University
Richards, Roy Jr.	2	State University of West Georgia
Salem, M. Ramez	2	University of Illinois at Chicago
Schuster, William M.	2	Gannon University
Slaner, Louella LaMer	2	Clarkson University
Tarrant, Richard & Amy	2	University of Vermont
Tate, Jack P.	2	College of Charleston
Wu, Frances	2	University of Southern California
Rudd, Mason & Mary	1	University of Louisville
Andreas, Lowell & Nadine	1	Mankato State University (Minn.)
Cheheyl, Teve	1	Dartmouth College
Smith, The Family of David C.	1	University of Wisconsin at Madison
Prizer, Charles J. & Dorothy	1	University of Illinois at Urbana-Champaign
MacAllister, Pershing E. & Becky	1	Carroll College (Wis.)
Slifka, Alan B. & Family	1	Brandeis University (Mass.)
Nitschke, Norman	1	University of Toledo
Wiekamp, Darwin & Dorothy	1	Indiana University at South Bend
Lamb, Lawrence E.	1	Kansas University Endowment
Haas, Robert B. & Candice J.	1	Harvard Law School
Hayes, Mariam Cannon	1	Queens College (N.C.)
Hicks, Ann & David	1	University of South Florida
Pizzuti, Ronald	1	Kent State Unversity
Baraff, Jay	1	George Washington University
Raitt, Rosemary	1	Pepperdine University (Cal.)
Beavers, Dr. W. Robert	1	Southern Methodist University
Caylor, Lloyd, Family	1	Lincoln Memorial University

(continued)

Giver	Amount	Recipient
	(in millions of dollars)	
Chace, Elizabeth Zopfi & Malcolm G.	1	Brown University
Geffen, David	1	Aids Action Council
Kobacker, Arthur J. & Sara Jo	1	United Way of Palm Beach County
Hambrecht, Sarah P. & William R.	1	Morehouse College
Dunn, Lloyd & Leota	1	Vanderbilt University
Kummer, Fred S. & June	1	University of Missouri at Rolla
Morgan, Perry	1	Chrysler Museum of Art
Hartzmak, Lee & Dolores and Family	1	Temple-Tifereth Israel
Holyfield, Evander	1	Windsor Village United Methodist Church
Robertson, Timothy B. & Lisa Nelson	1	University of Virginia
Speh, Albert J.	1	Fenwick High School
Cross, Wright W. & Annie Rea	1	University of Southern Mississippi
Kelly, Paul K.	1	University of Pennsylvania
Emilson, C. Herbert & Pauline	1	Wildlands Trust of Southeastern Massachusetts
Self, Madison & Lila	1	Kansas University

Top 75 American Charities, Ranked by Amount of Private Support, 1997
(Source: *The Chronicle of Philanthropy*, 1997 Survey)

Name of Charity	Private Support (in millions of dollars)
Salvation Army	1,012
American Cancer Society	511
American Red Cross	479
Catholic Charities USA	388
Second Harvest	351
YMCA of the USA	340
Habitat for Humanity International	334
Boys & Girls Clubs of America	327
American Heart Association	273
YWCA of the USA	265
Boy Scouts of America	233
Gifts In Kind International	223
Shriners Hospitals for Crippled Children	220
Campus Crusade for Christ International	213

(continued)

Name of Charity	Private Support (in millions of dollars)
Nature Conservancy	204
World Vision	185
St. Jude's Children's Research Hospital	174
Children's Miracle Network (Osmond Foundation)	141
United Jewish Appeal	139
March of Dimes Birth Defects Foundation	139
Goodwill Industries International	137
Feed the Children (Larry Jones International Ministries Inc.)	126
Planned Parenthood Federation of America	123
Muscular Dystrophy Association	114
National Easter Seal Society	112
Big Brothers/Big Sisters of America	104
Christian Broadcasting Network	100
American Lung Association	100
Girl Scouts of the United States of America	95
Focus on the Family	94
National Multiple Sclerosis Society	94
Project HOPE	93
Christian Children's Fund	90
Disabled American Veterans	90
United Negro College Fund	90
Billy Graham Evangelistic Association	89
Wycliffe Bible Translators	89
Arthritis Foundation	88
American Diabetes Foundation	81
Trinity Broadcasting Network	80
Junior Achievement	78
Paralyzed Veterans	78
Covenant House	68
Father Flanagan's Boys' Home (Boys Town)	68
Compassion International	68
The Navigators	63
Cystic Fibrosis Foundation	61
Catholic Relief Services	60
Young Life	57
City of Hope	56
Children International	55
Brother's Brother Foundation	53
U.S. Committee for UNICEF	52
Ducks Unlimited	50
Food for the Poor	50
Leukemia Society of America	49
World Wildlife Fund	48
Save the Children	48
Juvenile Diabetes Foundation International	48
Catholic Foreign Mission Society of America (Maryknoll)	47

(continued)

Name of Charity	Private Support (in millions of dollars)
Food for the Hungry	46
CARE	46
United Cerebral Palsy Associations	45
Christian Aid Ministries	43
Christian and Missionary Alliance	42
International Aid	40
Christian Appalachian Project	39
Mothers Against Drunk Driving	36
Moody Bible Institute of Chicago	36
Children's Mercy Hospital	35
Christian Relief Services	32
Volunteers of America	30
Childreach Plan International	29
In Touch Ministries	28
American Bible Society	27

Top Ten Corporate Givers in Each Major Category of Giving, 1996
(Source: *Foundation Giving Watch,* The Taft Group)

Category & Name of Corporation	Amount Donated (in thousands)
Arts & Humanities	
IBM Corp.	10,200
Mobil Oil Corp.	10,182
Dayton Hudson Corp.	9,584
General Electric Co.	6,777
Chrysler Corp.	6,500
Boeing Corp.	6,000
Ameritech Co.	5,100
Ford Motor Co.	5,090
Citibank N.A.	4,820
Sara Lee Corp.	4,531
Civic & Community Affairs	
AT&T Corp.	14,400
Fannie Mae Corp.	11,626
Citibank N.A.	9,327
Mobil Oil Corp.	7,164
IBM Corp.	6,400
General Motors Corp.	6,300
General Electric Co.	5,980
Saint Paul Cos.	5,239
Johnson & Johnson	4,900
Ford Motor Co.	4,887

(continued)

Category & Name of Corporation	Amount Donated (in thousands)
Education	
Intel Corp.	46,961
IBM Corp.	43,900
Hewlett-Packard Co.	42,994
General Motors Corp.	34,000
Exxon Corp.	23,265
General Electric Co.	22,659
Procter & Gamble Co.	19,043
Microsoft Corp.	18,667
Merck & Co.	13,000
Ford Motor Co.	12,266
Environment	
Exxon Corp.	3,574
CIGNA Corp.	2,732
Chevron Corp.	2,000
IBM Corp.	1,700
Patagonia Inc.	1,200
General Motors Corp.	1,100
Hewlett-Packard Co.	652
Citibank	576
J. P. Morgan & Co.	520
Johnson & Johnson	514
Health	
Pfizer Inc.	75,225
Johnson & Johnson	63,100
Procter & Gamble Co.	21,337
General Motors Corp.	12,400
Sara Lee Corp.	12,048
Bristol-Myers Squibb Co.	9,036
Hewlett-Packard Co.	7,504
Eli Lilly & Co.	7,424
IBM Corp.	6,800
Ford Motor Co.	6,408
International	
Hewlett-Packard Co.	17,060
Exxon Corp.	13,014
Procter & Gamble Co.	9,741
IBM Corp.	8,500
General Motors Corp.	8,100
Johnson & Johnson	6,106
Citibank N.A.	4,773
Eli Lilly & Co.	4,707
E. I. duPont de Nemours	4,000
J. P. Morgan & Co.	3,494

(continued)

Category & Name of Corporation Amount Donated (in thousands)

Science (Top 5)

Procter & Gamble Co.	7,138
Intel Corp.	6,349
IBM Corp.	1,100
Gerber Products Co.	656
Medtronic Inc.	534

Social Services

Microsoft Corp.	17,869
IBM Corp.	17,400
General Electric Co.	10,026
J. C. Penney Co.	8,518
Boeing Co.	8,400
Dayton-Hudson Corp.	8,295
Ameritech Corp.	7,500
General Mills Inc.	6,555
US West Inc.	6,206
Amoco Corp.	6,100

Top Ten Foundation Givers in Each Major Category of Giving, 1996

(Source: *Foundation Giving Watch,* The Taft Group)

Category & Name of Foundation	Amount Donated (in thousands)
Arts & Humanities	
Burnett Foundation	22,548
Robert W. Woodruff Foundation	20,100
Pew Charitable Trusts	19,271
Ford Foundation	18,833
Brown Foundation	18,071
Lila Wallace-Reader's Digest Fund	18,042
Kresge Foundation	16,593
Andrew W. Mellon Foundation	15,909
John D. and Catherine T. MacArthur Foundation	13,553
John S. and James L. Knight Foundation	12,673
Civic & Community Affairs	
Ford Foundation	130,067
Lilly Endowment	76,200
John D. and Catherine T. MacArthur Foundation	36,953
Charles Stewart Mott Foundation	29,113

(continued)

Category & Name of Foundation	Amount Donated (in thousands)
McKnight Foundation	29,055
Alfred P. Sloan Foundation	26,028
Andrew W. Mellon Foundation	25,622
W. K. Kellogg Foundation	22,812
Pew Charitable Trusts	16,604
Rockefeller Foundation	15,723

Education

Howard Hughes Medical Institute	77,033
Annenberg Foundation	71,569
W. K. Kellogg Foundation	65,171
Andrew W. Mellon Foundation	62,290
Donald W. Reynolds Foundation	54,922
Lilly Endowment	45,400
Duke Endowment	39,469
Ford Foundation	37,667
W. M. Keck Foundation	36,255
Pew Charitable Trusts	29,925

Environment

John D. and Catherine T. MacArthur Foundation	34,359
David and Lucile Packard Foundation	25,337
Richard King Mellon Foundation	24,230
Pew Charitable Trusts	22,997
Ford Foundation	16,733
Charles Stewart Mott Foundation	11,707
W. Alton Jones Foundation	11,672
Andrew W. Mellon Foundation	9,703
Robert W. Woodruff Foundation	6,225
William Penn Foundation	6,047

Health

Robert Wood Johnson Foundation	266,917
Robert W. Woodruff Foundation	206,052
W. K. Kellogg Foundation	50,254
Pew Charitable Trusts	46,218
California Endowment	31,908
Donald W. Reynolds Foundation	25,288
David and Lucile Packard Foundation	23,788
Henry J. Kaiser Family Foundation	23,550
Duke Endowment	18,992
Kate B. Reynolds Charitable Trust	13,045

International

Rockefeller Foundation	70,927
W. K. Kellogg Foundation	70,075
Ford Foundation	44,000

(continued)

Category & Name of Foundation	Amount Donated (in thousands)
John D. and Catherine T. MacArthur Foundation	28,920
Open Society Institute-New York	27,752
Charles Stewart Mott Foundation	10,121
W. Alton Jones Foundation	8,337
Rockefeller Brothers Fund	5,124
Henry Luce Foundation	5,076
Howard Hughes Medical Institute	3,474

Religion (Top 5)

Lilly Endowment	45,000
Richard and Helen DeVos Foundation	15,700
Pew Charitable Trusts	13,035
Koch Foundation	10,220
Raskob Foundation for Catholic Activities	5,050

Science

David and Lucile Packard Foundation	35,788
Whitaker Foundation	17,632
Arnold and Mabel Beckman Foundation	9,100
Alfred P. Sloan Foundation	6,819
Carnegie Corp. of New York	6,575
McKnight Foundation	4,833
Research Corp.	4,818
Camille and Henry Dreyfus Foundation	3,902
Whitehall Foundation	2,489
Atlantic Foundation	1,206

Social Services

Ford Foundation	90,633
Harry and Jeanette Weinberg Foundation	41,040
McKnight Foundation	20,781
William Penn Foundation	16,966
Richard King Mellon Foundation	16,032
Kresge Foundation	13,445
J. E. and L. E. Mabee Foundation	11,037
David and Lucile Packard Foundation	10,166
Dewitt Wallace-Reader's Digest Fund	8,693
Ewing Marion Kauffman Foundation	8,512

NOTES

CHAPTER 1. COUNTING OUR SOCIAL CAPITAL

1. Survey by *Los Angeles Times*, January 19–22, 1995.

CHAPTER 2. NATION OF LONERS?

1. Robert D. Putnam, "Bowling Alone: America's Declining Social Capital," *The Journal of Democracy*, January 1995, p. 77. Putnam subsequently extended his argument: "The Strange Disappearance of Civic America," *The American Prospect*, Winter 1996, pp. 34–48; and "Tuning In, Tuning Out: The Strange Disappearance of Social Capital in America," *PS: Political Science and Politics*, December 1995, pp. 664–683.

2. Professor Putnam will have his scholarly say in a forthcoming book.

3. Much of the coverage has been in the form of short journalistic pieces, but there have been a few efforts made to look at these issues in greater depth. For example, an entire issue of *American Behavioral Scientist* was devoted to "Social Capital, Civil Society and Contemporary Democracy." See Volume 40, Number 5, March/April 1997, edited by Bob Edwards and Michael W. Foley. Greater depth was also provided through a conference, "Is Civil Society Weakening? A Look at the Evidence," sponsored by the Pew Charitable Trusts, the National Commission on Civic Renewal, and the Brookings Institution (November 1996).

4. For a sampling of some of the more thoughtful statements of civic decline arguments, see Robert Bellah, Richard Madsen, and William Sullivan, "Individualism and the Crisis of Civic Membership," *The Christian Century*, May 8, 1996, pp. 510–515; John Brehm and Wendy Rahn, "Individual Level Evidence for the Causes and Consequences of Social Capital," *American Journal of Political Science* (forthcoming); David S. Broder, "Civic Life and Civility," *The Washington Post*, January 1, 1995, p. C7; William A. Galston, "Won't You Be My Neighbor?" *The American Prospect*, May/June 1996, pp. 16–18; Richard Morin and Dan Baltz, "Americans Losing Trust in Each Other and Institutions; Suspicion of

Strangers Breeds Widespread Cynicism," *The Washington Post*, January 28, 1996, p. A1; William Raspberry, "Our Declining Civic-Mindedness," *The Washington Post*, December 2, 1994, p. A31; Paul Starr, "The Disengaged," *The American Prospect*, Fall 1995, pp. 7–8; Eric M. Uslaner, "Faith, Hope and Charity: Social Capital, Trust and Collective Action" (College Park, MD: University of Maryland, 1995, unpublished manuscript); and George Will, "Declining Social Connectedness," *The Atlanta Journal and Constitution*, January 5, 1995, p. A12.

5. Neal R. Peirce, "Civic America: We Aren't That Bad," *The Plain Dealer*, February 11, 1996. See, too, Robert J. Samuelson, "'Bowling Alone' Is Bunk," *The Washington Post*, April 10, 1996; Michael Schudson, "What If Civic Life Didn't Die?" *The American Prospect*, March/April 1996, pp. 17–20; Andrew Greeley, "Coleman Revisited: Religious Structures as a Source of Social Capital," *American Behavioral Scientist*, March/April 1997, pp. 587–594; idem, "The Other Civic America: Religion and Social Capital," *The American Prospect*, May/June 1997, pp. 68–73; and John Clark, "Shifting Engagements: Lessons From the 'Bowling Alone' Debate," *Hudson Briefing Paper*, October 1996, pp. 1–16. My colleagues and I also contributed to the critical example by devoting much of an issue of the Roper Center's magazine, *The Public Perspective* (June/July 1996), to the topic.

6. Quoted by Peirce in "Civic America: We Aren't That Bad."

7. Nicholas Lemann, "Kicking in Groups," *The Atlantic Monthly*, April 1996, p. 26.

8. Theda Skocpol, "Unravelling From Above," *The American Prospect*, March/April 1996, pp. 21, 23.

9. Skocpol, p. 25.

10. George F. Will, "Look at All the Lonely Bowlers," *The Washington Post*, January 5, 1995, p. A29.

11. Alexis de Tocqueville, *Democracy in America* (New York: Vintage Books, 1990), Vol. 2, p. 108.

12. See, for example, Robert A. Nisbet, *Community and Power* (New York: Oxford University Press, 1962).

13. Following the brutal totalitarian experience of the 1930s and then World War II, social scientists explored the importance of an active and independent associational life in sustaining pluralism and democracy—and the determined effort of totalitarian regimes to eradicate all groups not aligned with the regime. See, for example, William Kornhauser, *The Politics of Mass Society* (Glencoe, IL: The Free Press, 1959). Kornhauser argued that "a plurality of independent and limited-function groups supports liberal democracy by providing social bases of

free and open competition for leadership, widespread participation in the selection of leaders, restraint in the application of pressures on leaders, and self-government in wide areas of social life. Therefore, where social pluralism is strong, liberty and democracy tend to be strong; and conversely, forces which weaken social pluralism also weaken liberty and democracy" (pp. 230–231).

14. John Brandl, "Can Such a Nation of Individuals Try to Live as a Community?" *The Star Tribune,* January 23, 1995, p. 7A. Amitai Etzioni's journal, *The Responsive Community,* has been an important outlet for communitarian thinking. See also by Etzioni, *The New Golden Rule: Community and Morality in a Democratic Society* (New York: Basic Books, 1996); and, as editor, his *New Communitarian Thinking: Persons, Virtues, Institutions, and Communities* (Charlottesville: University Press of Virginia, 1995). See, too, the work of communitarian philosopher Alasdair MacIntyre, *After Virtue: A Study in Moral Theory,* 2nd ed. (Notre Dame, IN: University of Notre Dame Press, 1984); and Michael Sandel, *Democracy's Discontent: America in Search of a Public Philosophy* (Cambridge, MA: Belknap Press of Harvard University, 1996).

15. Brandl, p. 7A.

16. Robert L. Woodson, Sr., *The Triumphs of Joseph: How Today's Community Healers Are Reviving Our Streets and Neighborhoods* (New York: The Free Press, 1998).

17. Michael Novak, *The Fire of Invention: Civil Society and the Future of the Corporation* (Lanham, MD: Rowman & Littlefield Publishers, 1997), pp. 14–15.

18. Ibid., p. 9.

19. Peter F. Drucker, *The Ecological Vision: Reflections on the American Condition* (New Brunswick, NJ: Transaction Publishers, 1993), p. 9.

20. Edward C. Banfield, *The Moral Basis of a Backward Society* (New York: The Free Press, 1958), p. 10.

21. Ibid., pp. 83–84.

22. Tocqueville, Vol. 2, pp. 106–107.

23. Tocqueville, Vol. 1, p. 307.

24. Tocqueville, Vol. 2, p. 115.

25. Ibid.

26. Daniel Bell, *The Coming of Postindustrial Society* (New York: Basic Books, 1973), pp. 20, 44.

27. Lester M. Salamon and Helmut K. Anheier, "The Civil Society Sector," *Society,* January/February 1997, p. 60.

CHAPTER 3.   FROM BOWLING LEAGUES TO SOCCER NATION

1. Everett Ladd and Karlyn Bowman, *Attitudes Toward the Environment: Twenty-Five Years After Earth Day* (Washington, DC: The AEI Press, 1995), p. 50.

2. Robert D. Putnam, "Bowling Alone: America's Declining Social Capital," p. 77.

3. George Pettinico, "Civic Participation Alive and Well in Today's Environmental Groups," *The Public Perspective*, June/July 1996, p. 27.

4. Ibid.

5. Ibid., p. 28.

6. See, for a recitation of this argument, Laura M. Litvan, "Is the PTA Now a Teacher's Pet? Close Ties to Unions Spur Some to Break Away," *Investor's Business Daily*, October 20, 1997, pp. A1, A40.

7. Roger Finke and Rodney Stark, *The Churching of America, 1776–1990* (New Brunswick, NJ: Rutgers University Press, 1994), p. 16.

8. See, for discussion of the movement to independent, nondenominational community churches, Charles Trueheart, "Welcome to the Next Church: Megachurch Trend," *The Atlantic Monthly*, August 1996, pp. 37–58.

9. Ibid., p. 42.

10. Ibid.

11. Ibid., p. 37.

12. See "The We Decade: Rebirth of Community," *Dallas Morning News*, a series published March 5, 1995, to May 19, 1996.

13. J. Miller McPherson, "Hypernetwork Sampling: Duality and Differentiation Among Voluntary Associations," *Social Networks*, Vol. 3, 1982, pp. 225–249; and by McPherson and Thomas Rotolo, "Testing a Dynamic Model of Social Composition: Diversity and Change in Voluntary Groups," *American Sociological Review*, April 1996, pp. 179–201.

14. I've described these tendencies across the economy and the polity in "The 1994 Congressional Elections: The Postindustrial Realignment Continues," *Political Science Quarterly*, Spring 1995.

15. Little League Web pages.

16. Web pages of the American Youth Soccer Organization and of the Oswego Youth Soccer Association.

17. Lemann, "Kicking in Groups," p. 25.

18. See Sidney Verba, Kay Lehman Schlozman, and Henry Brady, *Voice and*

Equality: Civic Voluntarism in American Politics (Cambridge, MA: Harvard University Press, 1995), pp. 58–65.

19. Putnam, "Tuning In, Tuning Out," p. 666.

20. Frank R. Baumgartner and Jack L. Walker, "Survey Research and Membership in Voluntary Associations," *American Journal of Political Science*, November 1988, p. 924.

21. Ibid.

22. Tom Smith, "Trends in Voluntary Group Membership: Comments on Baumgartner and Walker," *American Journal of Political Science*, August 1990, pp. 641–661.

CHAPTER 4.   VOLUNTEERING AND GIVING

1. Tocqueville, *Democracy in America*, Vol. 1, p. 41.

2. Ibid., p. 44.

3. Surveys by Princeton Survey Research Associates for the Pew Research Center. The national survey was conducted February 6–9, 1997. The Philadelphia survey was conducted November 13–December 11, 1996.

4. See my "The Twentysomethings: 'Generation Myths' Revisited," *The Public Perspective*, January/February 1994, pp. 14–18 and 88–96. Subsequent to this article, *Reader's Digest* commissioned me to conduct a new national survey on the generations issue. That study was done in August 1994 and reported on in *Reader's Digest* a few months later: Ladd, "Exposing the Myth of the Generation Gap," January 1995, pp. 49–54.

5. The Girl Scouts' category "adult members" is essentially the same as "volunteers." The former term is used because it includes a small percentage of paid staff members holding Girl Scout membership.

6. Gerald Gamm and Robert Putnam, "Association Building in America, 1840–1940," unpublished manuscript.

7. Arthur M. Schlesinger, "Biography of a Nation of Joiners," *The American Historical Review*, October 1944, p. 1.

8. Ibid., p. 2.

9. Ibid.

10. Ibid., p. 5.

11. From Tocqueville's diary, as quoted by George Wilson Pierson, *Tocqueville and Beaumont in America* (New York: Oxford University Press, 1938), p. 479.

12. William E. Channing, "Remarks on Associations," *The Christian Examiner*, September 1829, p. 139.

13. Schlesinger, "Biography of a Nation of Joiners," p. 16.

14. Ibid., p. 20.

15. Ibid., p. 21.

CHAPTER 5.   SOCIAL CONFIDENCE AND TRUST

1. Putnam, "Bowling Alone," p. 73.

2. Ibid. Emphasis added.

3. I reviewed some of the arguments and relevant survey data in "The Polls: The Question of Confidence," *The Public Opinion Quarterly*, Winter 1976–1977, pp. 544–552.

4. Historian David Potter is the foremost proponent of the argument that relative material abundance has distinguished American experience, in particular creating a special sense of national place and confidence. See David M. Potter, *People of Plenty: Economic Abundance and the American Character* (Chicago: University of Chicago Press, 1954).

5. Ezra Vogel's *Japan as Number 1: Lessons for the United States* (Cambridge, MA: Harvard University Press, 1979) helped give economic alarmism enormous currency.

6. In 1995, for example, *The Washington Post* convened a group of prominent politicians, economists, and pollsters, including Treasury Secretary Robert Rubin, then-senator Bill Bradley, and former housing and urban development secretary and Republican presidential hopeful Jack Kemp, to discuss the income inequality issue. The group's conclusion was summarized by the headline "Income Gap Is Issue Number 1, Debaters Agree," *The Washington Post*, December 7, 1995.

7. The quotation cited above is from an interview with Secretary Reich reported in the *Chicago Tribune*, June 23, 1995.

8. Stanley Greenberg, "Private Heroism and Public Purpose," *The American Prospect*, September/October 1996, pp. 34–40. See, too, by Greenberg, *Middle-Class Dreams: The Politics and Power of the New American Majority* (New York: Times Books, 1995).

9. Remarks made at a roundtable discussion at the American Enterprise Institute for Public Policy Research, November 21, 1996, as quoted in Everett Ladd and Karlyn Bowman, *Attitudes Toward Economic Inequality* (Washington, DC: AEI Press, 1998), p. 44.

10. James Davison Hunter and Daniel C. Johnson, "A State of Disunion?" *The Public Perspective*, February/March 1997, p. 37.

11. Curtis Gans, "Pollyanna's America," *The Washington Post*, August 6, 1997, p. A19.

12. Ibid.

13. Ladd, "The Polls: The Question of Confidence."

14. Ibid., p. 552.

15. Peter Bruce, "How the Experts Got 1996 Voter Turnout Wrong," *The Public Perspective,* October/November 1997, p. 41.

16. Ivor Crewe, "Electoral Participation," in *Democracy at the Polls: A Comparative Study of Competitive National Election,* edited by David Butler, Howard R. Penniman, and Austin Ranney (Washington, DC: American Enterprise Institute, 1981), p. 232.

17. Bruce, "How the Experts Got 1996 Voter Turnout Wrong," p. 40.

18. James Davison Hunter et al., "The 1996 Survey of American Political Culture," *The Public Perspective,* February/March 1997, p. 8.

19. The National Opinion Research Center, General Social Surveys, 1973, 1996.

20. Herbert Croly, *The Promise of American Life* (New Brunswick, NJ: Transaction Publishers, 1993; first published in 1909).

CHAPTER 6. IN COMPARATIVE PERSPECTIVE

1. Channing, "Remarks on Associations," p. 139.

2. Henry Watterson, quoted in John P. Davis, *Corporations: A Study of the Origin and Development of Great Business Combinations* (New York: G. P. Putnam's Sons, 1905), pp. 1, 4n.

3. See in particular, in Lipset's extensive work on American exceptionalism, his assessment of voluntary group engagement: *American Exceptionalism: A Double-Edged Sword* (New York: W. W. Norton & Company, Inc., 1996), pp. 276–281. See, too, in his earlier seminal work, *The First New Nation: The United States in Historical and Comparative Perspective* (New York: W. W. Norton & Company, 1979), his discussion of voluntary associations in a comparative context, pp. 159–169.

4. Walter Dean Burnham, "The 1980 Earthquake: Realignment, Reaction, or What?" in Thomas Ferguson and Joel Rogers, eds., *The Hidden Election: Politics and Economics in the 1980 Presidential Campaign* (New York: Pantheon Books, 1981), p. 132.

5. Peter F. Drucker, *The Ecological Vision: Reflections on the American Condition* (New Brunswick, NJ: Transaction Publishers, 1993), p. 6.

6. Lipset, *The First New Nation,* pp. 160–161.

7. An American Gentleman (Calvin Colton), *A Voice From America to England* (London: Henry Colburn, 1839), pp. 87–88, 97.

8. Drucker, *The Ecological Vision: Reflections on the American Condition*, p. 9.

9. Lester M. Salamon and Helmut K. Anheier, "The Civil Society Sector," *Society*, January/February 1997, p. 60.

10. Virginia A. Hodgkinson, "Civic Participation in America: Volunteering and Contributing," *The Public Perspective*, March/April 1994, p. 14.

11. Helmut K. Anheier, Lester M. Salamon, and Edith Archambault, "Participating Citizens: U.S.-Europe Comparisons in Volunteer Action," *The Public Perspective*, March/April 1994, p. 16.

12. Salamon and Anheier, "The Civil Society Sector," p. 61.

13. Ibid.

14. Ibid., pp. 63–64.

15. For Robert Nisbet's own words on the subject, see his *Community and Power* (New York: Oxford University Press, 1962).

16. Salamon and Anheier, "The Civil Society Sector," p. 61.

17. Ibid., pp. 64–65.

AFTERWORD

1. James Bryce, *The American Commonwealth*, Vol. 1 (New York, London: Macmillan and Co., 1983–95), p. 1.

2. G. K. Chesterton, *What I Saw in America* (New York: Dodd, Mead, and Company, 1922; reprinted in 1968 by Da Capo Press), p. 7.

3. Ibid., p. 17.

4. Auberon Waugh, "A Tremendous Trifle," Preface to *The Complete Father Brown* (New York: Dodd, Mead, 1982), p. viii.

5. Ibid., pp. 16–17.

6. Speech delivered in Springfield, Illinois, on June 26, 1957. The entire text may be found in *Abraham Lincoln: Speeches and Writings, 1832–1858* (New York: The Library of America, 1989).

7. Robert Bellah et al., *Habits of the Heart* (Berkeley, CA: University of California Press, 1985).

8. Mary Ann Glendon, *Rights Talk: The Impoverishment of Political Discourse* (New York: The Free Press, 1991), p. x.

9. Robert H. Bork, *Slouching Towards Gomorrah: Modern Liberalism and American Decline* (New York: Regan Books, 1996).

10. Jeffrey W. Hayes and Seymour Martin Lipset, "Individualism: A Double-Edged Sword," *The Responsive Community*, Winter 1993/94, p. 80.

APPENDIX 1.   "ON THE ROLE AND IMPORTANCE OF ASSOCIATIONS IN AMERICA"

1. Alexis de Tocqueville, *Democracy in America* (New York: Vintage Books, 1990), Vol. 1, pp. 191–192.

2. Alexis de Tocqueville, *Democracy in America,* Vol. 2, 1990, pp. 106–107.

3. Tocqueville, Vol. 2, p. 110.

4. Tocqueville, Vol. 1, pp. 303–304.

5. Ibid., pp. 305–306.

6. Ibid., p. 307.

7. Tocqueville, Vol. 2, p. 115.

8. Ibid., p. 119.

9. Tocqueville, Vol. 1, p. 195.

10. Tocqueville, Vol. 2, p. 108.

THE STATE OF AMERICA'S CIVIC ENGAGEMENT

A Bibliography

An American Gentleman (Calvin Colton). *A Voice from America to England.* London: Henry Colburn, 1839.

Anderson, Leith. *A Church for the 21st Century.* Minneapolis: Bethany House Publishers, 1992.

Anheier, Helmut K., Lester M. Salamon, and Edith Archambault. "Participating Citizens: U.S.-Europe Comparisons in Volunteer Action." *The Public Perspective.* March–April 1994: 16–18, 34.

Babchuk, Nicholas, and Alan Booth. "Voluntary Association Membership: A Longitudinal Analysis." *American Sociological Review.* February 1969: 31–45.

Banfield, Edward C. *The Moral Basis of a Backward Society.* New York: The Free Press, 1958.

Bass, Melissa. "Towards a New Theory and Practice of Civic Education: An Evaluation of Public Achievement." Master's thesis. University of Minnesota. May, 1995.

Baumgartner, Frank R., and Jack L. Walker. "Survey Research and Membership in Voluntary Associations." *American Journal of Political Science.* November 1988: 908–928.

Bell, Daniel. *The Coming of Postindustrial Society.* New York: Basic Books, 1973.

Bellah, Robert, et al. *Habits of the Heart.* Berkeley, CA: University of California Press, 1985.

Bellah, Robert, Richard Madsen, and William Sullivan. "Individualism and the Crisis of Civic Membership." *The Christian Century.* May 8, 1996: 510–515.

Berkowitz, Peter. "The Art of Association." *The New Republic.* June 24, 1996: 44–49.

Bork, Robert H. *Slouching Towards Gomorrah: Modern Liberalism and American Decline.* New York: Regan Books, 1996.

Bradley, Martin B., et al. *Churches and Church Membership in the United States, 1990.* Atlanta, GA: Glenmary Research Center, 1992.

Brehm, John, and Wendy Rahn. "Individual Level Evidence for the Causes and Consequences of Social Capital." *American Journal of Political Science.* Forthcoming.

Bremner, Robert H. *American Philanthropy.* Chicago: University of Chicago Press, 1988.

———. *Giving, Charity and Philanthropy in History.* New Brunswick, NJ: Transaction Publishers, 1996.

Broder, David S. "Civic Life and Civility." *The Washington Post.* January 1, 1995: C7.

Bruce, Peter. "How the Experts Got 1996 Voter Turnout Wrong Last Year." *The Public Perspective.* October–November 1997: 39–43.

Bryce, James. *The American Commonwealth.* Volumes 1 and 2. New York: Macmillan and Company, 1983–95. First published in London in 1888 by Macmillan and Company.

Butler, David, Howard R. Penniman, and Austin Ranney, editors. *Democracy at the Polls: A Comparative Study of Competitive National Elections.* Washington, DC: American Enterprise Institute, 1981.

Channing, William E. "Remarks on Associations." *The Christian Examiner.* September, 1829.

Chesterton, G. K. *What I Saw in America.* New York: Dodd, Mead, and Company, 1922. Reprinted in 1968 by Da Capo Press.

Clark, John. "Shifting Engagements: Lessons from the 'Bowling Alone' Debate." *Hudson Briefing Paper.* Indianapolis: Hudson Institute, October 1996: 1–16.

Clemens, Elisabeth S. *The People's Lobby: Organizational Innovation and the Rise of Interest Group Politics in the United States, 1890–1925.* Chicago: University of Chicago Press, Spring 1977.

Coleman, Lee. "What is America? A Study of Alleged American Traits." *Social Forces*. Vol. 19(4), 1941: 492–499.

Crewe, Ivor. "Electoral Participation," in *Democracy at the Polls: A Comparative Study of Competitive National Elections*. Edited by David Butler, Howard R. Penniman, and Austin Ranney. Washington, D.C.: American Enterprise Institute, 1981.

Croly, Herbert. *The Promise of American Life*. New Brunswick, NJ: Transaction Publishers, 1993. First published in 1909.

Curti, Merle. *American Philanthropy Abroad: A History*. New Brunswick, NJ: Rutgers University Press, 1963.

Curtis, James E., Edward G. Grabb, and Douglas E. Baer. "Voluntary Association Membership in Fifteen Countries: A Comparative Analysis." *American Sociological Review*. April 1992: 139–152.

Dahl, Robert A. "The Problem of Civic Competence." *Journal of Democracy*. October 1992: 45–59.

Dionne, E. J., Jr. "Can Government Nurture Civic Life?" *Brookings Review*. Fall 1996: 3–5.

Drucker, Peter F. *The Ecological Vision: Reflections on the American Condition*. New Brunswick, NJ: Transaction Publishers, 1993.

————. *Managing The Non-Profit Organization*. New York: HarperCollins, 1990.

Edwards, Patricia Klobus, John N. Edwards, and Ann DeWitt Watts. "Women, Work, and Social Participation." *Journal of Voluntary Action Research*. January–March 1984: 7–22.

Edwards, Robert, and Michael W. Foley, editors. "Social Capital, Civil Society, and Contemporary Democracy." *American Behavioral Scientist*. March–April 1997.

Etzioni, Amitai. *The New Golden Rule: Community and Morality in a Democratic Society*. New York: Basic Books, 1996.

————, editor. *New Communitarian Thinking: Persons, Virtues, Institutions, and Communities*. Charlottesville: University Press of Virginia, 1995.

Finke, Roger, and Rodney Stark. *The Churching of America, 1776–1990*. New Brunswick, NJ: Rutgers University Press, 1994.

Fukuyama, Francis. *Trust, the Social Virtues and the Creation Of Prosperity*. New York: The Free Press, 1995.

Galston, William A. "Won't You Be My Neighbor?" *The American Prospect*. May–June 1996: 16–18.

Gamm, Gerald, and Robert Putnam. "Association Building in America, 1840–1940." Unpublished manuscript.

Gans, Curtis. "Pollyanna's America." *The Washington Post.* August 6, 1997: A19.

Gaskin, Katharine, and Justin Davis Smith. "A New Civic Europe?" Volunteer Centre. London, UK. Unpublished manuscript.

Gillman, Nicholas Paine. *Socialism and the American Spirit.* Boston: Houghton, Mifflin and Company, 1893.

Glendon, Mary Ann. *Rights Talk: The Impoverishment of Political Discourse.* New York: The Free Press, 1991.

Greeley, Andrew. "Coleman Revisited: Religious Structures as a Source of Social Capital." *American Behavioral Scientist.* March–April 1997: 587–594.

———. "The Other Civic America: Religion and Social Capital." *The American Prospect.* May–June 1997: 68–73.

Greenberg, Stanley. *Middle Class Dreams: The Politics and Power of the New American Majority.* New York: Times Books, 1995.

———. "Private Heroism and Public Purpose." *The American Prospect.* September–October 1996: 34–40.

Haar, Charlene K. "Cutting Class: The PTA Plays Hooky From Educational Reform." *Policy Review.* Summer 1995: 86–90.

———. "Why the PTA Doesn't Represent Parents." *Insight on the News.* March 27, 1996: 18–20.

Hall, Peter Dobkin. "Founded on the Rock, Built Upon Shifting Sands: Churches, Voluntary Associations, and Nonprofit Organizations in Public Life, 1850–1990." Unpublished paper. Program on Non-Profit Organizations, Yale University.

Hartz, Louis. *The Liberal Tradition in America.* New York: Harcourt, Brace & World, 1955.

Hayes, Jeffrey W., and Seymour Martin Lipset. "Individualism: A Double-Edged Sword." *The Responsive Community.* Winter 1993/94: 80.

Hayghe, Howard V. "Volunteers in the U.S: Who Donates the Time?" *Monthly Labor Review.* February 1991: 17–23.

Hodgkinson, Virginia A. "Civic Participation in America: Volunteering and Contributing." *The Public Perspective.* March–April 1994: 14–15.

Hunter, James Davison, and Daniel C. Johnson. "A State of Disunion?" *The Public Perspective,* February–March 1997: 37.

Hyman, H., and C. R. Wright. "Trends in Voluntary Association Memberships of American Adults: Replication Based on Secondary Analysis of National Sample Surveys." *American Sociological Review.* April 1971: 191–206.

Knoke, David, and R. Thomason. "Voluntary Association Membership Trends and the Family Life Cycle." *Social Forces.* Vol. 56(1), 1977: 48–65.

Kornhauser, William. *The Politics of Mass Society.* Glencoe, IL: The Free Press, 1959.

Ladd, Everett C. *The American Ideology: An Exploration of the Origins, Meaning, and Role of American Political Ideas.* Monograph series #1. Storrs, CT: The Roper Center for Public Opinion Research, 1994.

———. "The Data Just Don't Show Erosion of America's 'Social Capital.'" *The Public Perspective.* June–July 1996: 1, 5–22.

———. "Exposing the Myth of the Generation Gap." *Reader's Digest.* January 1995: 49–54.

———. "The Polls: The Question of Confidence." *Public Opinion Quarterly.* Winter 1976/77: 544–552.

———. "The Twentysomethings: 'Generation Myths' Revisited." *The Public Perspective.* January–February 1994: 14–18.

Ladd, Everett C., and Karlyn Bowman. *Attitudes Towards the Environment: Twenty-Five Years After Earth Day.* Washington, DC: AEI Press, 1995.

———. *Attitudes Toward Economic Inequality.* Washington, DC: AEI Press, 1998.

Lawrence, Jill. "Wanted: Good Citizens, Close Communities." *USA Today.* December 16, 1996.

Lemann, Nicholas. "Kicking in Groups." *The Atlantic Monthly.* April 1996: 22–26.

Lipset, Seymour Martin. *American Exceptionalism: A Double-Edged Sword.* New York: W. W. Norton & Co., 1996.

———. *The First New Nation: The United States in Historical and Comparative Perspective.* New York: W. W. Norton & Co., 1979.

———. "Why No Socialism in the United States?" in S. Bialer and S. Sluzar, editors, *Sources of Contemporary Radicalism.* Boulder, CO: Westview Press, 1977.

Litvan, Laura M. "Is the PTA Now a Teacher's Pet?: Close Ties to Unions Spur Some to Break Away." *Investor's Business Daily.* October 20, 1997: A1, A40.

MacIntyre, Alasdair. *After Virtue: A Study in Moral Theory.* Second edition. Notre Dame, IN: University of Notre Dame Press, 1984.

Martz, Arnold C. *The Generosity of Americans: Its Source, Its Achievements.* Englewood Cliffs, NJ: Prentice Hall, 1966.

McPherson, J. Miller. "Hypernetwork Sampling: Duality and Differentiation Among Voluntary Associations." *Social Networks.* Volume 3, 1982: 225–249.

McPherson, J. Miller, and Thomas Rotolo. "Testing a Dynamic Model of Social Composition: Diversity and Change in Voluntary Groups." *American Sociological Review.* April 1996: 179–201.

Morin, Richard, and Dan Baltz. "Americans Losing Trust in Each Other and Institutions: Suspicion of Strangers Breeds Widespread Cynicism." *The Washington Post.* January 28, 1996: A1.

Nayyar, Seema. "The More We Give." *Newsweek.* December 18, 1995.

Nielsen, Waldemar A. *Inside American Philanthropy.* Norman, OK: University of Oklahoma Press, 1996.

Nisbet, Robert A. *Community and Power.* New York: Oxford University Press, 1962.

Novak, Michael. *The Fire of Invention: Civil Society and the Future of the Corporation.* New York: Rowman & Littlefield, 1997.

Ostrower, Francie. *Why the Wealthy Give: The Culture of Elite Philanthropy.* Princeton, NJ: Princeton University Press, 1995.

Peirce, Neal R. "Civic America: We Aren't That Bad." *The Plain Dealer.* February 11, 1996.

Pettinico, George. "Civic Participation Alive and Well in Today's Environmental Groups." *The Public Perspective.* June/July 1996: 27–30.

Piven, Frances Fox, and Richard A. Cloward. *Why Americans Don't Vote.* New York: Pantheon Books, 1988.

Potter, David M. *People of Plenty: Economic Abundance and the American Character.* Chicago: University of Chicago Press, 1954.

Putnam, Robert D. "Bowling Alone: America's Declining Social Capital." *Journal of Democracy.* January 1995: 65–78.

———. *Making Democracy Work: Civic Traditions in a Modern Italy.* Princeton, NJ: Princeton University Press, 1993.

———. "The Strange Disappearance of Civic America." *The American Prospect.* Winter 1996: 34–48.

———. "Tuning In, Tuning Out: The Strange Disappearance of Social Capital in America." *PS: Political Science & Politics.* December 1995: 644–683.

Raspberry, William. "Our Declining Civic-Mindedness." *The Washington Post.* December 2, 1994: A31.

Rosenstone, Steven J., and John Mark Hansen. *Mobilization, Participation, and Democracy in America.* New York: Macmillan, 1993.

Salamon, Lester, M. *Partners in Public Service.* Baltimore: Johns Hopkins University Press, 1995.

Salamon, Lester M., and Helmut K. Anheier. "The Civil Society Sector." *Society.* January–February 1997: 60–65.

————. *The Emerging Nonprofit Sector.* New York: St. Martin's Press, 1996.

Samson, Leon. "Americanism as Surrogate Socialism," in Leon Samson, *Toward a United Front.* New York: Farrar and Rinehart, 1935.

Samuelson, Robert J. "'Bowling Alone' Is Bunk." *The Washington Post.* April 10, 1996.

Sandel, Michael. *Democracy's Discontent: America in Search of a Public Philosophy.* Cambridge, MA: Belknap Press of Harvard University, 1996.

Schervish, Paul G. "The Dependent Variable of the Independent Sector: A Research Agenda for Improving the Definition and Measurement of Giving and Volunteering." *International Journal of Voluntary and Nonprofit Organizations.* August 1993: 223–232.

Schlesinger, Arthur M. "Biography of a Nation of Joiners." *The American Historical Review.* October 1944: 1–25.

Schneewind, J. B. *Giving: Western Ideas of Philanthropy.* Indiana University Press, 1996.

Schneider, Barbara, and James S. Coleman. *Parents, Their Children, and Schools.* Boulder, CO: Westview Press, 1993.

Schudson, Michael. "What If Civic Life Didn't Die?" *The American Prospect.* March–April 1996: 17–28.

Skocpol, Theda. "Unravelling From Above." *The American Prospect.* March–April 1996: 21–25.

Smith, Tom W. "Factors Relating to Misanthropy in Contemporary American Society." *GSS Topical Report.* June 1996.

————. "Trends in Voluntary Group Membership: Comments on Baumgartner and Walker." *American Journal of Political Science.* August 1990: 641–661.

Starr, Paul. "The Disengaged." *The American Prospect.* Fall 1995: 7–8.

Stengel, Richard. "Bowling Together." *Time.* July 22, 1996: 35–36.

"The Solitary Bowler." *The Economist.* February 1995: 21–22.

Tocqueville, Alexis de. *Democracy in America.* Volumes 1 and 2. New York: Vintage Books, 1990. First published in 1835 in France.

Truehart, Charles. "Welcome to the Next Church: Megachurch Trend." *The Atlantic Monthly.* August 1996: 37–58.

Uslaner, Eric M. "Faith, Hope and Charity: Social Capital, Trust and Collective Action." College Park, MD: University of Maryland. 1995. Unpublished manuscript.

Verba, Sidney, Kay Lehman Schlozman, and Henry E. Brady. *Voice and Equality: Civic Voluntarism in American Politics.* Cambridge, MA: Harvard University Press, 1995.

Voss, Kim. *The Making of American Exceptionalism.* Ithaca, NY: Cornell University Press, 1993.

Waugh, Auberon. "A Tremendous Trifle." Preface to *The Complete Father Brown.* New York: Dodd, Mead, 1982.

"The We Decade: Rebirth of Community." *Dallas Morning News.* A series published March 5, 1995, to May 19, 1996.

Whitfill, Kathryn. "Don't Fault the OET in the Nation's PTAs." *Insight on the News.* March 27, 1995: 21–22.

Will, George F. "Declining Social Connectedness." *The Atlanta Journal and Constitution.* January 5, 1995: A12.

———. "Look at All the Lonely Bowlers." *The Washington Post.* January 5, 1995: A29.

Woodson, Robert L., Sr. *The Triumphs of Joseph: How Today's Community Healers Are Reviving Our Streets and Neighborhoods.* New York: The Free Press, 1998.

Wuthnow, Robert, and Virginia A. Hodgkinson, editors. *Faith and Philanthropy in America.* San Francisco: Jossey-Bass Publishers, 1990.

INDEX